TOTAL

DELIVERANCE

VOLUME 1

(ANOINTED PRAYERS TO BREAK YOKES & CURSES)

Timothy Atunnise

TSA SOLUTION PUBLISHING
ATLANTA, GEORGIA

TOTAL DELIVERANCE – VOLUME 1

Copyright © 2014 by Timothy Atunnise

All rights reserved. No part of this book may be reproduced, copied, stored or transmitted in any form or by any means – graphic, electronic, or mechanical, including photocopying, recording, or information storage and retrieval systems without the prior written permission of TSA Solution Publishing except where permitted by law.

Unless otherwise specified, all Scripture quotations in this book are from The Holy Bible, King James Version. KJV is Public domain in the United States printed in 1987.

GLOVIM PUBLICATIONS
1078 Citizens Parkway
Suite A
Morrow, GA 30260 USA.
glovimpublications@gmail.com
www.glovimonline.org

TSA Solution Publishing
A division of Timat Store, LLC.
Atlanta, GA 30294
timatstore@yahoo.com

Cover Design: Tim Atunnise

Printed in the United States of America

DEDICATION

This book is dedicated to my wonderful wife Becky, thank you for being my friend and partner; and for your unconditional love and unending support. Your prayer, counsel and support are priceless, thank you for always being there.
May the Lord continue to increase your anointing, wisdom, and every knowledge in the name of Jesus Christ.

To my Lord Jesus Christ:
Thank you for the mercy and grace you extend
to someone like me.

IMPORTANT NOTICE

Deliverance is a benefit of the Kingdom, only for the children of God. If you have not accepted Jesus Christ as your personal Lord and Savior, this is the best time to do so.

Before you continue, you need to be sure you are in the right standing with God if you want to exercise authority and power in the name of Jesus Christ. The Bible says,

"Then he called his twelve disciples together, and gave them power and authority over all devils, and to cure diseases." - Luke 9:1

"And these signs shall follow them that believe; in my name shall they cast out devils; they shall speak with new tongues; they shall take up serpents; and if they drink any deadly thing, it shall not hurt them; they shall lay hands on the sick, and they shall recover." – Mark 16:17-18.

These are promises for the Children of God, not just for everyone. Why don't you give your life to Christ today and you will have access to the same promises. Food that is meant for the children will not be given to the dogs.

"But he answered and said, it is not meet to take the children's bread, and cast it to dogs" – Matthew 15:26.

If you really want to be delivered from any bondage of the wicked and be set free from any form of captivity, I ask you today to give your life to Christ. If you are ready, say this prayer with all your heart:

"Dear Heavenly Father, You have called me to Yourself in the name of Your dear Son Jesus Christ. I realize that Jesus Christ is the only Way, the Truth, and the Life.

I acknowledge to You that I am a sinner. I believe that Your only begotten Son Jesus Christ shed His precious blood on the cross, died for my sins, and rose again on the third day. I am truly sorry for the deeds which I have committed against You, and therefore, I am willing to repent (turn away from my sins). Have mercy on me, a sinner. Cleanse me, and forgive me of my sins.

I truly desire to serve You, Lord Jesus. Starting from now, I pray that You would help me to hear Your still small voice. Lord, I desire to be led by Your Holy Spirit so I can faithfully follow You and obey all of Your commandments. I ask You for the strength to love You more than anything else so I won't fall back into my old ways. I also ask You to bring genuine believers into my life who will encourage me to live for You and help me stay accountable.

Jesus, I am truly grateful for Your grace which has led me to repentance and has saved me from my sins. By the indwelling of Your Holy Spirit, I now have the power to overcome all sin which before so easily entangled me. Lord Jesus, please transform my life so that I may bring glory and honor to You alone and not to myself.

Right now I confess Jesus Christ as the Lord of my life. With my heart, I believe that God the Father raised His Son Jesus Christ from the dead. This very moment I acknowledge that Jesus Christ is my Savior and according to His Word, right now I am born again. Thank You Jesus, for coming into my life and hearing my prayer. I ask all of this in the name of my Lord and Savior, Jesus Christ. Amen".

I hereby congratulate and welcome you into the Kingdom. You hereby have full access to the benefits, promises and blessings of the Kingdom.

This book is loaded with blessings, you will not be disappointed as you continue to enjoy the goodness of the Lord.

INSTRUCTIONS

If you are new to this method of prayer, please follow this instruction carefully:

Step 1:

Spend enough time in praising and worshiping God not just for what He is about to do or what He has done, but WHO HE IS.

Step 2:

Unforgiveness will surely hinder your prayer, take time to remember all those who have done you wrong, and forgive them from the bottom of your heart. THIS IS VERY IMPORTANT BECAUSE YOUR DELIVERANCE DEPENDS ON IT.

Step 3:

Believe in your heart that God will answer your prayer when you call upon Him, and do not doubt in your heart.

Step 4:

Pray in the name of Jesus Christ alone.

Step 5:

Repeat each prayer point 25 to 30 times or until you are convinced that you receive answer before you go to the next prayer point. **Example:** When you take prayer point number 1, you say this prayer over and over again, 25 – 30 times or until you are convinced that you have an answer before you go to prayer point number 2.

Step 6:

It will be more effective if you can follow the instruction and do these prayers with fasting according to each section of this prayer program. If you want total deliverance from your bondage, take 5 or 7 days of sacrifice in fasting as you say your prayer aggressively, asking your situation to receive permanent solution and YOUR DELIVERANCE WILL BE MADE PERFECT IN THE NAME OF JESUS CHRIST. AMEN!

ATTENTION!!!

THIS KIND OF FAST IS WITHOUT FOOD AND WATER FROM SUNRISE TO SUNSET, THAT MEANS FROM MORNING TO 6PM IN THE EVENING.

Table of Contents

Dedication 3
Important Notice 4
Instructions 7

Deliverance from ancestral curses of poverty & empty pocket
Generational repentance 15
Deliverance from ancestral poverty 22
Breaking the curse of empty pocket 28
Prayer to end financial drought 35
Prayer to break curses attacking your finances 40
Deliverance from stronghold of lack & poverty 47
Deliverance from financial struggle 53

Deliverance from ancestral curses of rejection
Generational repentance 61
Deliverance from satanic attacks 68
Deliverance from ancestral curses of rejection 74
Prayer to erase marks of rejection 81
Prayer to overcome fear of rejection 86
Deliverance from foundational rejection 92
Prayer to cancel evil pronouncement 97

Deliverance from generational curses of failure
Generational repentance 105
Prayer to break cycle of failure 112
Prayer against last minute failure 117
Deliverance from the spirit of almost there 123
Deliverance from ancestral curse of failure 129

9

Deliverance from curses of untimely death
Generational repentance 137
Deliverance from the curse of untimely death 144
Deliverance from power of the grave 151
Breaking cycle of sudden death 159
I shall not die but live 165

Deliverance from frustration
Generational repentance 173
Deliverance from curses of frustration 180
Prayer to stop ancestral evil flow 185
Prayer for supernatural turn-around 191
No more frustration 197

Deliverance from ancestral curses of marital delay
Generational repentance 205
Breaking ancestral curses of marital delay 212
O Lord, I am tired of waiting 218
Breaking soul-ties 224
Prayer to erase evil marks 230
Breaking stronghold of marital delay 236
I shall not make mistake 242

Deliverance from ancestral curses of tragedy
Generational repentance 249
Prayer to destroy roots of sorrow 256
Deliverance from ancestral curse of tragedy 261
I shall cry no more 268
There shall be no evil report 274

"And one of the multitude answered and said, Master, I have brought unto thee my son, which hath a dumb spirit; And wheresoever he taketh him, he teareth him: and he foameth, and gnasheth with his teeth, and pineth away: and I spake to thy disciples that they should cast him out; and they could not. He answereth him, and saith, O faithless generation, how long shall I be with you? how long shall I suffer you? bring him unto me.

And they brought him unto him: and when he saw him, straightway the spirit tare him; and he fell on the ground, and wallowed foaming. And he asked his father, How long is it ago since this came unto him? And he said, Of a child. And ofttimes it hath cast him into the fire, and into the waters, to destroy him: but if thou canst do any thing, have compassion on us, and help us.

Jesus said unto him, If thou canst believe, all things are possible to him that believeth. And straightway the father of the child cried out, and said with tears, Lord, I believe; help thou mine unbelief. When Jesus saw that the people came running together, he rebuked the foul spirit, saying unto him, Thou dumb and deaf spirit, I charge thee, come out of him, and enter no more into him. And the spirit cried, and rent him sore, and came out of him: and he was as one dead; insomuch that many said, He is dead. But Jesus took him by the hand, and lifted him up; and he arose.

And when he was come into the house, his disciples asked him privately, Why could not we cast him out? And he said unto them, This kind can come forth by nothing, but by prayer and fasting." – Mark 9:17-29

DELIVERANCE FROM ANCESTRAL CURSES OF POVERTY & EMPTY POCKET

(7 DAYS FASTING & INTENSIVE PRAYER)

KEY BIBLE PASSAGE

"Now therefore thus saith the LORD of hosts; Consider your ways. Ye have sown much, and bring in little; ye eat, but ye have not enough; ye drink, but ye are not filled with drink; ye clothe you, but there is none warm; and he that earneth wages earneth wages to put it into a bag with holes.

Thus saith the LORD of hosts; Consider your ways. Go up to the mountain, and bring wood, and build the house; and I will take pleasure in it, and I will be glorified, saith the LORD. Ye looked for much, and, lo it came to little; and when ye brought it home, I did blow upon it. Why? saith the LORD of hosts. Because of mine house that is waste, and ye run every man unto his own house.

Therefore the heaven over you is stayed from dew, and the earth is stayed from her fruit. And I called for a drought upon the land, and upon the mountains, and upon the corn, and upon the new wine, and upon the oil, and upon that which the ground bringeth forth, and upon men, and upon cattle, and upon all the labour of the hands." – Haggai 1:5-11

DAY ONE

GENERATIONAL REPENTANCE

Passages To Read Before You Pray:
Exodus 20:1-5, Jeremiah 31:27-34, Daniel 9:1-19, Psalms 89

I stand on the word of God to claim my right as a child of the Kingdom, I cover myself in the blood of Jesus Christ, I cover my household and everything concerning me in the blood of Jesus Christ. I hereby charge this atmosphere by the blood of Jesus Christ and by the fire of the Holy Ghost. I command fresh fire of God to rest upon me now as in the day of Pentecost, let fresh anointing and new oil be released upon me now as I pray. I receive power and authority over the power and the kingdom of darkness, to root out and to pull down, to destroy and to throw down, to build and to plant; whatever I decree in this prayer shall be established; whatever I bind today shall be bound in heaven and whatever I loose today shall be loosed in heaven as it is written in the word of God. Let fresh fire of God be released on my prayer altar and my prayer life now, prince of Persia cannot hinder my prayer, territorial spirit of my neighborhood cannot hinder my prayer, household wickedness cannot hinder my prayer.

I can see my prayer attracting divine intervention. This is the day that the Lord has made, I will rejoice and be glad in it. This is the day that the Lord has chosen to set me free from any form of

bondage and break any form of curses upon my life; this is the day that I will receive a total and complete deliverance in every area of my life, today shall mark the beginning of a new thing in my life.

I am a child of God, born of the Spirit, redeemed by the blood of the Lamb. It is written concerning me that power and authority is given unto me over all devils and to cure diseases, I hereby take authority over any form of curses upon my life, be it ancestral, be it generational, be it demon-inflicted or self-inflicted; I command all curses upon my life to break now by the authority in the name of Jesus Christ. The Bible says, where the word of a king is, there is power; today I speak as a king with the authority and power of the King of kings, and I command every other power to bow in the name of Jesus Christ. I render any power behind any curse upon my life useless and ineffective; I overcome any form of distraction, spiritual laziness and slumber, before the end of this prayer session my testimonies shall manifest without delay by the power in the name of Jesus Christ. Amen!

PRAYER POINTS

1. O God my Father, thank you for being my God, my Father and my friend.
2. O God my Father, thank you for the privilege to know you and the power of the resurrection of Jesus Christ.
3. O God my Father, thank you for always being there for me and with me.
4. O God my Father, thank you for the great and mighty things that you are doing in my life.

5. O God my Father, thank you for your provision and protection over me and my household.
6. O God my Father, thank you for always answering my prayers.
7. O God my Father, I come in the name of Jesus Christ to repent for the sins and transgressions of my ancestors, forgive us and cleanse us by the blood of Jesus Christ.
8. O God my Father, I repent today for all disobedience of your commands by turning away and listening to the enemy, forgive me O Lord and cleanse me by the blood of Jesus Christ.
9. O God my Father, I repent today for all disobedience of your commands by turning away and listening to people instead of you, forgive me O Lord and cleanse me by the blood of Jesus Christ.
10. O God my Father, I repent today for all disobedience of your commands by turning away and listening to my own voice instead of your voice, forgive me O Lord and cleanse me by the blood of Jesus Christ.
11. O God my Father, I repent today for anyone in my family line who offered sacrifices that were not favorable and right, forgive us O Lord and cleanse us by the blood of Jesus Christ.
12. O God my Father, I repent today for withholding of the first-fruits and the best portion of my harvest, forgive me O Lord and cleanse me by the blood of Jesus Christ.
13. O God my Father, I repent today for all wrong motives and attitudes of heart concerning all of my giving; forgive me O Lord and cleanse me by the blood of Jesus Christ.

14. O God my Father, I repent today for all my anger and resentment, forgive me O Lord and cleanse me by the blood of Jesus Christ.
15. O God my Father, I repent today for all bloodshed committed by my ancestors, forgive us O Lord and let the blood of Jesus Christ speak mercy on our behalf, in the name of Jesus Christ.
16. O God my Father, I repent today for all my ancestors who denied justice to the poor, forgive us O Lord and cleanse us by the blood of Jesus Christ.
17. O God my Father, I repent today for all my ancestors who withheld forgiveness against anyone, forgive us today O Lord and cleanse us by the blood of Jesus Christ.
18. O God my Father, I repent today for shutting my ears to the cry of the poor, forgive me O Lord and cleanse me by the blood of Jesus Christ.
19. O God my Father, I repent today for all of my sins and my ancestors' for exploitation of the poor, forgive us today O Lord and cleanse us by the blood of Jesus Christ.
20. O God my Father, I repent today for any generational dishonesty, even the smallest hidden, accepted, or self-justified dishonesty, forgive us O Lord and cleanse us by the blood of Jesus Christ.
21. O God my Father, I repent today for any of my ancestors who would not forgive debts in the Lord's timing and who ignored the poor, forgive us today and cleanse us by the blood of Jesus Christ.
22. O God my Father, I repent today for all hardheartedness, tightfistedness, and selfishness, forgive me today and cleanse me by the blood of Jesus Christ.

23. O God my Father, I repent today for any of my ancestors who were unfaithful, greedy, disobedient, thieves or liars, forgive us O Lord and cleanse us by the blood of Jesus Christ.
24. O God my Father, I repent today for breaking the covenant and coveting or keeping the things of the pagans and not totally destroying them as commanded, forgive us today and cleanse us by the blood of Jesus Christ.
25. O God my Father, I repent today for all my ancestors who were evil and tried to control and frustrate the poor, forgive us O Lord and cleanse us by the blood of Jesus Christ.
26. O God my Father, I repent today for ignoring discipline and correction, forgive me Lord and cleanse me by the blood of Jesus Christ.
27. I disassociate myself from all evil done by my ancestors by the power in the blood of Jesus Christ.
28. I disassociate myself from all evil attitudes done by my ancestors against the will and purpose of God, in the name of Jesus Christ.
29. With all my heart I disagree with all sins committed by my ancestors, Father Lord have mercy and cleanse me by the blood of Jesus Christ.
30. Today with all my heart I declare that I refuse to be like my parents, in the name of Jesus Christ.
31. Today with all my heart I declare that I refuse to be like any of my ancestors, in the name of Jesus Christ.
32. I refuse to suffer the same problems as my parents, I reject it; my heart, soul, spirit and body reject it in the name of Jesus Christ.

33. I refuse to suffer the same problems as any of my ancestors, I reject it; my heart, soul, spirit and body reject it in the name of Jesus Christ.
34. In the name of Jesus Christ, I refuse to go through what my parents went through, my case is different, I am a child of God and covered by the blood of Jesus Christ.
35. By the power and authority in the blood of Jesus Christ, I sever myself from my bloodline, in the name of Jesus Christ.
36. By the power and authority in the blood of Jesus Christ, I sever myself from the connection to any of my ancestors, in the name of Jesus Christ.
37. By the power and authority in the blood of Jesus Christ, I sever myself from spiritual connection to any of my ancestors, in the name of Jesus Christ.
38. By the power and authority in the blood of Jesus Christ, I sever myself from physical connection to any of my ancestors, in the name of Jesus Christ.
39. By the power and authority in the blood of Jesus Christ, I sever myself from emotional connection to any of my ancestors, in the name of Jesus Christ.
40. By the power and authority in the blood of Jesus Christ, I sever myself from mental connection to any of my ancestors, in the name of Jesus Christ.
41. By the power and authority in the blood of Jesus Christ, I sever myself from the connection to the idol of my father's house, in the name of Jesus Christ.
42. By the power and authority in the blood of Jesus Christ, I sever myself from the connection to the idol of my mother's house, in the name of Jesus Christ.

43. By the power and authority in the blood of Jesus Christ, I destroy every spiritual DNA that links me to my ancestors by the fire of God, in the name of Jesus Christ.
44. By the power and authority in the blood of Jesus Christ, I destroy every spiritual DNA that links my children to my ancestors by the fire of God, in the name of Jesus Christ.
45. O God my Father, grant me grace not to follow the sinful path of my ancestors, I will do your will and follow your precepts in the name of Jesus Christ.

DAY TWO

DELIVERANCE FROM ANCESTRAL POVERTY

Passages To Read Before You Pray:
Job 36:11, Psalms 35, 118, Galatians 3:13

I stand on the word of God to claim my right as a child of the Kingdom, I cover myself in the blood of Jesus Christ, I cover my household and everything concerning me in the blood of Jesus Christ. I hereby charge this atmosphere by the blood of Jesus Christ and by the fire of the Holy Ghost. I command fresh fire of God to rest upon me now as in the day of Pentecost, let fresh anointing and new oil be released upon me now as I pray. I receive power and authority over the power and the kingdom of darkness, to root out and to pull down, to destroy and to throw down, to build and to plant; whatever I decree in this prayer shall be established; whatever I bind today shall be bound in heaven and whatever I loose today shall be loosed in heaven as it is written in the word of God. Let fresh fire of God be released on my prayer altar and my prayer life now, prince of Persia cannot hinder my prayer, territorial spirit of my neighborhood cannot hinder my prayer, household wickedness cannot hinder my prayer.

I can see my prayer attracting divine intervention. This is the day that the Lord has made, I will rejoice and be glad in it. This is the day that the Lord has chosen to set me free from any form of

bondage and break any form of curses upon my life; this is the day that I will receive a total and complete deliverance in every area of my life, today shall mark the beginning of a new thing in my life.

I am a child of God, born of the Spirit, redeemed by the blood of the Lamb. It is written concerning me that power and authority is given unto me over all devils and to cure diseases, I hereby take authority over any form of curses upon my life, be it ancestral, be it generational, be it demon-inflicted or self-inflicted; I command all curses upon my life to break now by the authority in the name of Jesus Christ. The Bible says, where the word of a king is, there is power; today I speak as a king with the authority and power of the King of kings, and I command every other power to bow in the name of Jesus Christ. I render any power behind any curse upon my life useless and ineffective; I overcome any form of distraction, spiritual laziness and slumber, before the end of this prayer session my testimonies shall manifest without delay by the power in the name of Jesus Christ. Amen!

PRAYER POINTS

1. O God my Father, thank you for being my God, my Father and my friend.
2. O God my Father, thank you for the privilege to know you and the power of the resurrection of Jesus Christ.
3. O God my Father, thank you for always being there for me and with me.
4. O God my Father, thank you for the great and mighty things that you are doing in my life.

5. O God my Father, thank you for your provision and protection over me and my household.
6. O God my Father, thank you for always answering my prayers.
7. I confess my sins before you today and I ask you to forgive me on the basis of your mercy, in the name of Jesus Christ.
8. Wash me clean today O Lord by the blood of Jesus Christ.
9. I cover myself and my household with the blood of Jesus Christ.
10. My prayers today will not go in vain; my prayers will produce the desired results in the name of Jesus Christ.
11. By the power and authority in the blood of Jesus Christ, I receive redemption from ancestral curses of poverty, in the name of Jesus Christ.
12. By the power and authority in the blood of Jesus Christ, I receive redemption from ancestral curses of lack, in the name of Jesus Christ.
13. By the power and authority in the blood of Jesus Christ, I break all curses of poverty in my bloodline from my life to my past generations all the way to Adam the first man, in the name of Jesus Christ.
14. By the power and authority in the blood of Jesus Christ, I break all curses of lack in my bloodline from my life to my past generations all the way to Adam the first man, in the name of Jesus Christ.
15. By the power and authority in the blood of Jesus Christ, I break all curses of never had enough in my bloodline from my life to my past generations all the way to Adam the first man, in the name of Jesus Christ.

16. By the power and authority in the blood of Jesus Christ, I break all curses of financial struggle in my bloodline from my life to my past generations all the way to Adam the first man, in the name of Jesus Christ.
17. By the power and authority in the blood of Jesus Christ, I break all curses of financial instability in my bloodline from my life to my past generations all the way to Adam the first man, in the name of Jesus Christ.
18. By the power and authority in the blood of Jesus Christ, I break all curses of empty pocket in my bloodline from my life to my past generations all the way to Adam the first man, in the name of Jesus Christ.
19. By the power and authority in the blood of Jesus Christ, I break all curses of hard labor no blessing in my bloodline from my life to my past generations all the way to Adam the first man, in the name of Jesus Christ.
20. By the power and authority in the blood of Jesus Christ, I break all curses of financial setback in my bloodline from my life to my past generations all the way to Adam the first man, in the name of Jesus Christ.
21. By the power and authority in the blood of Jesus Christ, I break all curses of financial embarrassment in my bloodline from my life to my past generations all the way to Adam the first man, in the name of Jesus Christ.
22. By the power and authority in the blood of Jesus Christ, I break all curses of empty bank account in my bloodline from my life to my past generations all the way to Adam the first man, in the name of Jesus Christ.
23. By the power and authority in the blood of Jesus Christ, I break all curses of inability to provide in my bloodline from my life to my past generations all the way to Adam the first man, in the name of Jesus Christ.

24. Every evil covenant that is directly responsible for financial hardship in my life; be revoked now by the power and authority in the name of Jesus Christ.
25. Every evil covenant that is directly responsible for financial difficulties in my life; be revoked now by the power and authority in the name of Jesus Christ.
26. Every evil covenant that is directly responsible for financial embarrassment in my life; be revoked now by the power and authority in the name of Jesus Christ.
27. Every evil covenant that is directly responsible for the curses of empty pocket in my life; be revoked now by the power and authority in the name of Jesus Christ.
28. Every evil covenant that is directly responsible for the curses of never had enough in my life; be revoked now by the power and authority in the name of Jesus Christ.
29. Every evil covenant that is directly responsible for the curses of poverty in my life; be revoked now by the power and authority in the name of Jesus Christ.
30. I bind all family curses of poverty and cast them out of my life now in the name of Jesus Christ.
31. I bind all family curses of poverty and cast them out of my home now in the name of Jesus Christ.
32. I bind all family curses of poverty and cast them out of my finances now in the name of Jesus Christ.
33. I break every satanic chain of poverty off my life, in the name of Jesus Christ
34. I renounce and reverse every financial curse upon my life by the power and authority in the blood of Jesus Christ.
35. I renounce and reverse every curse of empty pocket upon my life by the power and authority in the blood of Jesus Christ.

36. I renounce and reverse every curse of never had enough upon my life by the power and authority in the blood of Jesus Christ.
37. I renounce and reverse every curse of empty bank account upon my life by the power and authority in the blood of Jesus Christ.
38. I renounce and reverse every curse of financial embarrassment upon my life by the power and authority in the blood of Jesus Christ.
39. I renounce and reverse every curse of lack upon my life by the power and authority in the blood of Jesus Christ.
40. I renounce and reverse every curse of poverty upon my life by the power and authority in the blood of Jesus Christ.
41. I renounce and reverse every curse of fruitless hard-work upon my life by the power and authority in the blood of Jesus Christ.
42. I bind and destroy the activities of anti-harvest forces operating in my life by the power and authority in the name of Jesus Christ.
43. I bind and destroy the activities of anti-prosperity forces operating in my life by the power and authority in the name of Jesus Christ.
44. I bind and destroy the activities of anti-breakthrough forces operating in my life by the power and authority in the name of Jesus Christ.
45. I bind and destroy the activities of anti-miracle forces operating in my life by the power and authority in the name of Jesus Christ.

DAY THREE

BREAKING THE CURSE OF EMPTY POCKET

Passages To Read Before You Pray:
Haggai 1:5-11, Malachi 3:8-12, Psalms 30, 42, 86

I stand on the word of God to claim my right as a child of the Kingdom, I cover myself in the blood of Jesus Christ, I cover my household and everything concerning me in the blood of Jesus Christ. I hereby charge this atmosphere by the blood of Jesus Christ and by the fire of the Holy Ghost. I command fresh fire of God to rest upon me now as in the day of Pentecost, let fresh anointing and new oil be released upon me now as I pray. I receive power and authority over the power and the kingdom of darkness, to root out and to pull down, to destroy and to throw down, to build and to plant; whatever I decree in this prayer shall be established; whatever I bind today shall be bound in heaven and whatever I loose today shall be loosed in heaven as it is written in the word of God. Let fresh fire of God be released on my prayer altar and my prayer life now, prince of Persia cannot hinder my prayer, territorial spirit of my neighborhood cannot hinder my prayer, household wickedness cannot hinder my prayer.

I can see my prayer attracting divine intervention. This is the day that the Lord has made, I will rejoice and be glad in it. This is the day that the Lord has chosen to set me free from any form of

bondage and break any form of curses upon my life; this is the day that I will receive a total and complete deliverance in every area of my life, today shall mark the beginning of a new thing in my life.

I am a child of God, born of the Spirit, redeemed by the blood of the Lamb. It is written concerning me that power and authority is given unto me over all devils and to cure diseases, I hereby take authority over any form of curses upon my life, be it ancestral, be it generational, be it demon-inflicted or self-inflicted; I command all curses upon my life to break now by the authority in the name of Jesus Christ. The Bible says, where the word of a king is, there is power; today I speak as a king with the authority and power of the King of kings, and I command every other power to bow in the name of Jesus Christ. I render any power behind any curse upon my life useless and ineffective; I overcome any form of distraction, spiritual laziness and slumber, before the end of this prayer session my testimonies shall manifest without delay by the power in the name of Jesus Christ. Amen!

PRAYER POINTS

1. O God my Father, thank you for being my God, my Father and my friend.
2. O God my Father, thank you for the privilege to know you and the power of the resurrection of Jesus Christ.
3. O God my Father, thank you for always being there for me and with me.
4. O God my Father, thank you for the great and mighty things that you are doing in my life.

5. O God my Father, thank you for your provision and protection over me and my household.
6. O God my Father, thank you for always answering my prayers.
7. I confess my sins before you today and I ask you to forgive me on the basis of your mercy, in the name of Jesus Christ.
8. Wash me clean today O Lord by the blood of Jesus Christ.
9. I cover myself and my household with the blood of Jesus Christ.
10. My prayers today will not go in vain; my prayers will produce the desired results in the name of Jesus Christ.
11. Every device of the enemy to divert my wealth through sickness; be destroyed now by the fire of God, in the name of Jesus Christ.
12. Every device of the enemy to divert my wealth through sudden death; be destroyed now by the fire of God, in the name of Jesus Christ.
13. Every device of the enemy to divert my wealth through accidents; be destroyed now by the fire of God, in the name of Jesus Christ.
14. Every device of the enemy to divert my wealth through financial emergencies; be destroyed now by the fire of God, in the name of Jesus Christ.
15. Every handwriting of poverty upon my life; be completely wiped off by the blood of Jesus Christ.
16. Every handwriting of poverty upon my family; be completely wiped off by the blood of Jesus Christ.
17. Every handwriting of poverty upon my spouse; be completely wiped off by the blood of Jesus Christ.

18. Every handwriting of poverty upon my children; be completely wiped off by the blood of Jesus Christ.
19. Every handwriting of poverty upon my business; be completely wiped off by the blood of Jesus Christ.
20. Every handwriting of poverty upon my finances; be completely wiped off by the blood of Jesus Christ.
21. I command every leaking pocket, purse and wallet to be sealed now by the blood of Jesus Christ.
22. O God my Father, dispatch your warring angels to pursue, arrest and destroy any power anywhere building financial roadblocks in my pathway to prosperity, in the name of Jesus Christ.
23. O God my Father, dispatch your warring angels to pursue, arrest and destroy principalities and powers building financial roadblocks in my pathway to prosperity, in the name of Jesus Christ.
24. O God my Father, dispatch your warring angels to pursue, arrest and destroy household wickedness building financial roadblocks in my pathway to prosperity, in the name of Jesus Christ.
25. O God my Father, dispatch your warring angels to pursue, arrest and destroy witchcraft powers building financial roadblocks in my pathway to prosperity, in the name of Jesus Christ.
26. O God my Father, dispatch your warring angels to pursue, arrest and destroy any Jezebel spirit building financial roadblocks in my pathway to prosperity, in the name of Jesus Christ.
27. O God my Father, dispatch your warring angels to pursue, arrest and destroy any unfriendly friend building financial roadblocks in my pathway to prosperity, in the name of Jesus Christ.

28. By the power and authority in the blood of Jesus Christ, I pull down every financial roadblock in my pathway to prosperity, in the name of Jesus Christ.
29. By the power and authority in the blood of Jesus Christ, I declare today that the blood of Jesus Christ has broken every curse of lack in my life, in the name of Jesus Christ.
30. By the power and authority in the blood of Jesus Christ, I declare today that the blood of Jesus Christ has broken every curse of lack in my family, in the name of Jesus Christ.
31. By the power and authority in the blood of Jesus Christ, I declare today that the blood of Jesus Christ has broken every curse of lack in the life of my spouse, in the name of Jesus Christ.
32. By the power and authority in the blood of Jesus Christ, I declare today that the blood of Jesus Christ has broken every curse of lack upon my children, in the name of Jesus Christ.
33. By the power and authority in the blood of Jesus Christ, I declare today that the blood of Jesus Christ has broken every curse of lack upon my future generations, in the name of Jesus Christ.
34. By the power and authority in the blood of Jesus Christ, I declare today that the blood of Jesus Christ has broken every curse of poverty in my life, in the name of Jesus Christ.
35. By the power and authority in the blood of Jesus Christ, I declare today that the blood of Jesus Christ has broken every curse of poverty upon my spouse, in the name of Jesus Christ.

36. By the power and authority in the blood of Jesus Christ, I declare today that the blood of Jesus Christ has broken every curse of poverty upon my children, in the name of Jesus Christ.
37. By the power and authority in the blood of Jesus Christ, I declare today that the blood of Jesus Christ has broken every curse of poverty upon my future generations, in the name of Jesus Christ.
38. By the power and authority in the blood of Jesus Christ, I declare today that the blood of Jesus Christ has broken every curse of poverty in my finances, in the name of Jesus Christ.
39. By the power and authority in the blood of Jesus Christ, I declare today that the blood of Jesus Christ has broken every curse of poverty over my business, in the name of Jesus Christ.
40. By the power and authority in the blood of Jesus Christ, I declare today that the blood of Jesus Christ has broken every curse of poverty in every area of my interest, in the name of Jesus Christ.
41. By the power and authority in the blood of Jesus Christ, I declare today that the blood of Jesus Christ has broken every curse of empty pocket in my life, in the name of Jesus Christ.
42. By the power and authority in the blood of Jesus Christ, I declare today that the blood of Jesus Christ has broken every curse of empty pocket in my family, in the name of Jesus Christ.
43. By the power and authority in the blood of Jesus Christ, I declare today that the blood of Jesus Christ has broken every curse of empty pocket upon my spouse, in the name of Jesus Christ.

44. By the power and authority in the blood of Jesus Christ, I declare today that the blood of Jesus Christ has broken every curse of empty pocket upon my children, in the name of Jesus Christ.
45. By the power and authority in the blood of Jesus Christ, I declare today that the blood of Jesus Christ has broken every curse of empty pocket upon my future generations, in the name of Jesus Christ.

DAY FOUR

PRAYER TO END FINANCIAL DROUGHT

Passages To Read Before You Pray:
Joel 2:21-27, Philippians 4:19, Psalms 36, 132

I stand on the word of God to claim my right as a child of the Kingdom, I cover myself in the blood of Jesus Christ, I cover my household and everything concerning me in the blood of Jesus Christ. I hereby charge this atmosphere by the blood of Jesus Christ and by the fire of the Holy Ghost. I command fresh fire of God to rest upon me now as in the day of Pentecost, let fresh anointing and new oil be released upon me now as I pray. I receive power and authority over the power and the kingdom of darkness, to root out and to pull down, to destroy and to throw down, to build and to plant; whatever I decree in this prayer shall be established; whatever I bind today shall be bound in heaven and whatever I loose today shall be loosed in heaven as it is written in the word of God. Let fresh fire of God be released on my prayer altar and my prayer life now, prince of Persia cannot hinder my prayer, territorial spirit of my neighborhood cannot hinder my prayer, household wickedness cannot hinder my prayer.

I can see my prayer attracting divine intervention. This is the day that the Lord has made, I will rejoice and be glad in it. This is the day that the Lord has chosen to set me free from any form of

bondage and break any form of curses upon my life; this is the day that I will receive a total and complete deliverance in every area of my life, today shall mark the beginning of a new thing in my life.

I am a child of God, born of the Spirit, redeemed by the blood of the Lamb. It is written concerning me that power and authority is given unto me over all devils and to cure diseases, I hereby take authority over any form of curses upon my life, be it ancestral, be it generational, be it demon-inflicted or self-inflicted; I command all curses upon my life to break now by the authority in the name of Jesus Christ. The Bible says, where the word of a king is, there is power; today I speak as a king with the authority and power of the King of kings, and I command every other power to bow in the name of Jesus Christ. I render any power behind any curse upon my life useless and ineffective; I overcome any form of distraction, spiritual laziness and slumber, before the end of this prayer session my testimonies shall manifest without delay by the power in the name of Jesus Christ. Amen!

PRAYER POINTS

1. O God my Father, thank you for being my God, my Father and my friend.
2. O God my Father, thank you for the privilege to know you and the power of the resurrection of Jesus Christ.
3. O God my Father, thank you for always being there for me and with me.
4. O God my Father, thank you for the great and mighty things that you are doing in my life.

5. O God my Father, thank you for your provision and protection over me and my household.
6. O God my Father, thank you for always answering my prayers.
7. I confess my sins before you today and I ask you to forgive me on the basis of your mercy, in the name of Jesus Christ.
8. Wash me clean today O Lord by the blood of Jesus Christ.
9. I cover myself and my household with the blood of Jesus Christ.
10. My prayers today will not go in vain; my prayers will produce the desired results in the name of Jesus Christ.
11. By the power and authority in the name of Jesus Christ, I declare today that season of famine in my life is over.
12. By the power and authority in the name of Jesus Christ, I declare today that season of famine in my family is over.
13. By the power and authority in the name of Jesus Christ, I declare today that season of famine in my marriage is over.
14. By the power and authority in the name of Jesus Christ, I declare today that season of famine in my home is over.
15. By the power and authority in the name of Jesus Christ, I declare today that season of famine in my finances is over.
16. By the power and authority in the name of Jesus Christ, I declare today that season of famine in my business is over.
17. By the power and authority in the name of Jesus Christ, I declare today that season of drought in my life is over.

18. By the power and authority in the name of Jesus Christ, I declare today that season of drought in my family is over.
19. By the power and authority in the name of Jesus Christ, I declare today that season of drought in my marriage is over.
20. By the power and authority in the name of Jesus Christ, I declare today that season of drought in my home is over.
21. By the power and authority in the name of Jesus Christ, I declare today that season of drought in my finances is over.
22. By the power and authority in the name of Jesus Christ, I declare today that season of drought in my business is over.
23. O God my Father, let your promise of blessings and fruitfulness be restored unto me, in the name of Jesus Christ.
24. Today O Lord, let every evil mark of poverty upon my life be removed by the blood of Jesus Christ.
25. Today O Lord, let every evil mark of poverty upon my family be removed by the blood of Jesus Christ.
26. Today O Lord, let every evil mark of poverty upon my spouse be removed by the blood of Jesus Christ.
27. Today O Lord, let every evil mark of poverty upon my children be removed by the blood of Jesus Christ.
28. O God my Father, let every evil mark of misfortune upon my life be removed now by the blood of Jesus Christ.
29. O God my Father, let every evil mark of misfortune upon my spouse be removed now by the blood of Jesus Christ.

30. O God my Father, let every evil mark of misfortune upon my children be removed now by the blood of Jesus Christ.
31. O God my Father, let every evil mark of financial setback upon my life be removed now by the blood of Jesus Christ.
32. I stand on the word of God and I command every curse of wandering upon my life to break by the power and authority in the name of Jesus Christ.
33. I stand on the word of God and I command every curse of wandering upon my spouse to break by the power and authority in the name of Jesus Christ.
34. I stand on the word of God and I command every curse of wandering upon my children to break by the power and authority in the name of Jesus Christ.
35. I stand on the word of God and I command every curse of wandering upon every member of my family to break by the power and authority in the name of Jesus Christ.
36. I stand on the word of God and I break all curses that send spiritual locusts and worms to destroy my harvests, in the name of Jesus Christ.
37. I stand on the word of God and I break all curses that send devourer into my finances, in the name of Jesus Christ.

DAY FIVE

PRAYER TO BREAK CURSES ATTACKING YOUR FINANCES

Passages To Read Before You Pray:
Psalms 59, 69, 70, Galatians 3:13, Ephesians 3:20

I stand on the word of God to claim my right as a child of the Kingdom, I cover myself in the blood of Jesus Christ, I cover my household and everything concerning me in the blood of Jesus Christ. I hereby charge this atmosphere by the blood of Jesus Christ and by the fire of the Holy Ghost. I command fresh fire of God to rest upon me now as in the day of Pentecost, let fresh anointing and new oil be released upon me now as I pray. I receive power and authority over the power and the kingdom of darkness, to root out and to pull down, to destroy and to throw down, to build and to plant; whatever I decree in this prayer shall be established; whatever I bind today shall be bound in heaven and whatever I loose today shall be loosed in heaven as it is written in the word of God. Let fresh fire of God be released on my prayer altar and my prayer life now, prince of Persia cannot hinder my prayer, territorial spirit of my neighborhood cannot hinder my prayer, household wickedness cannot hinder my prayer.

I can see my prayer attracting divine intervention. This is the day that the Lord has made, I will rejoice and be glad in it. This is the

day that the Lord has chosen to set me free from any form of bondage and break any form of curses upon my life; this is the day that I will receive a total and complete deliverance in every area of my life, today shall mark the beginning of a new thing in my life.

I am a child of God, born of the Spirit, redeemed by the blood of the Lamb. It is written concerning me that power and authority is given unto me over all devils and to cure diseases, I hereby take authority over any form of curses upon my life, be it ancestral, be it generational, be it demon-inflicted or self-inflicted; I command all curses upon my life to break now by the authority in the name of Jesus Christ. The Bible says, where the word of a king is, there is power; today I speak as a king with the authority and power of the King of kings, and I command every other power to bow in the name of Jesus Christ. I render any power behind any curse upon my life useless and ineffective; I overcome any form of distraction, spiritual laziness and slumber, before the end of this prayer session my testimonies shall manifest without delay by the power in the name of Jesus Christ. Amen!

PRAYER POINTS

1. O God my Father, thank you for being my God, my Father and my friend.
2. O God my Father, thank you for the privilege to know you and the power of the resurrection of Jesus Christ.
3. O God my Father, thank you for always being there for me and with me.

4. O God my Father, thank you for the great and mighty things that you are doing in my life.
5. O God my Father, thank you for your provision and protection over me and my household.
6. O God my Father, thank you for always answering my prayers.
7. I confess my sins before you today and I ask you to forgive me on the basis of your mercy, in the name of Jesus Christ.
8. Wash me clean today O Lord by the blood of Jesus Christ.
9. I cover myself and my household with the blood of Jesus Christ.
10. My prayers today will not go in vain; my prayers will produce the desired results in the name of Jesus Christ.
11. By the power and authority in the blood of Jesus Christ, I command all curses attacking my finances to break now in the name of Jesus Christ.
12. By the power and authority in the blood of Jesus Christ, I command all curses attacking my sources of income to break now in the name of Jesus Christ.
13. By the power and authority in the blood of Jesus Christ, I command all curses attacking my pocket to break now in the name of Jesus Christ.
14. By the power and authority in the blood of Jesus Christ, I command all curses attacking my job to break now in the name of Jesus Christ.
15. By the power and authority in the blood of Jesus Christ, I command all curses attacking my business to break now in the name of Jesus Christ.

16. By the power and authority in the blood of Jesus Christ, I command all curses attacking my bank accounts to break now in the name of Jesus Christ.
17. By the power and authority in the blood of Jesus Christ, I command all curses attacking my helpers to break now in the name of Jesus Christ.
18. By the power and authority in the blood of Jesus Christ, I command all curses attacking my blessings to break now in the name of Jesus Christ.
19. By the power and authority in the blood of Jesus Christ, I command all curses attacking my prosperity to break now in the name of Jesus Christ.
20. By the power and authority in the blood of Jesus Christ, I command all curses attacking my financial miracles to break now in the name of Jesus Christ.
21. By the power and authority in the blood of Jesus Christ, I command all curses attacking my breakthrough to break now in the name of Jesus Christ.
22. By the power and authority in the blood of Jesus Christ, I command all curses attacking my financial freedom to break now in the name of Jesus Christ.
23. By the power and authority in the blood of Jesus Christ, I command all curses attacking my divine opportunity to break now in the name of Jesus Christ.
24. Every curse of poverty upon my life sponsored by the power of witchcraft, I command you to break now by the authority and power in the name of Jesus Christ.
25. Every curse of poverty upon my life sponsored by Pharaoh of my father's house, I command you to break now by the authority and power in the name of Jesus Christ.

26. Every curse of poverty upon my life sponsored by household wickedness, I command you to break now by the authority and power in the name of Jesus Christ.
27. Every curse of poverty upon my life sponsored by territorial spirit and power, I command you to break now by the authority and power in the name of Jesus Christ.
28. Every curse of poverty upon my life sponsored by unrepentant enemy, I command you to break now by the authority and power in the name of Jesus Christ.
29. Every curse of poverty upon my life sponsored by any satanic network, I command you to break now by the authority and power in the name of Jesus Christ.
30. Every curse that keeps me from enjoying the fruits of my labor, I command you to be removed permanently by the power and authority in the name of Jesus Christ.
31. Curses of poverty that have been passed on through my generation line, from Adam to me, I command you to break now by the power and authority in the name of Jesus Christ.
32. Curses of lack that have been passed on through my generation line, from Adam to me, I command you to break now by the power and authority in the name of Jesus Christ.
33. Curses of empty pocket that have been passed on through my generation line, from Adam to me, I command you to break now by the power and authority in the name of Jesus Christ.
34. Curses of financial instability that have been passed on through my generation line, from Adam to me, I command you to break now by the power and authority in the name of Jesus Christ.

35. Curses of financial embarrassment that have been passed on through my generation line, from Adam to me, I command you to break now by the power and authority in the name of Jesus Christ.
36. Curses of hard labor no blessing that have been passed on through my generation line, from Adam to me, I command you to break now by the power and authority in the name of Jesus Christ.
37. Curses of fruitless hard-work that have been passed on through my generation line, from Adam to me, I command you to break now by the power and authority in the name of Jesus Christ.
38. Curses of inability to provide that have been passed on through my generation line, from Adam to me, I command you to break now by the power and authority in the name of Jesus Christ.
39. Curses of never have enough that have been passed on through my generation line, from Adam to me, I command you to break now by the power and authority in the name of Jesus Christ.
40. O God my Father, bless me today with a new purse without holes in it, in the name of Jesus Christ.
41. I stand on the word of God and I command all crooked places of my financial life to be made perfectly straight, in the name of Jesus Christ.
42. I stand on the word of God and I command all the valleys of my financial life to be mightily exalted, in the name of Jesus Christ.
43. I stand on the word of God and I command all mountains of my financial life to be made plain, in the name of Jesus Christ.

44. I stand on the word of God and I command all my financial miracles to arrive speedily and be made manifest, in the name of Jesus Christ.
45. I stand on the word of God and I command all my financial deserts and wilderness to be turned into springs and pools overflowing with the waters of financial abundance and prosperity, in the name of Jesus Christ.

DAY SIX

DELIVERANCE FROM STRONGHOLD OF LACK & POVERTY

Passages To Read Before You Pray:
Obadiah 1:7, Isaiah 10:27, 2 Corinthians 10:3-6, Psalms 3, 9, 44

I stand on the word of God to claim my right as a child of the Kingdom, I cover myself in the blood of Jesus Christ, I cover my household and everything concerning me in the blood of Jesus Christ. I hereby charge this atmosphere by the blood of Jesus Christ and by the fire of the Holy Ghost. I command fresh fire of God to rest upon me now as in the day of Pentecost, let fresh anointing and new oil be released upon me now as I pray. I receive power and authority over the power and the kingdom of darkness, to root out and to pull down, to destroy and to throw down, to build and to plant; whatever I decree in this prayer shall be established; whatever I bind today shall be bound in heaven and whatever I loose today shall be loosed in heaven as it is written in the word of God. Let fresh fire of God be released on my prayer altar and my prayer life now, prince of Persia cannot hinder my prayer, territorial spirit of my neighborhood cannot hinder my prayer, household wickedness cannot hinder my prayer.

I can see my prayer attracting divine intervention. This is the day that the Lord has made, I will rejoice and be glad in it. This is the

day that the Lord has chosen to set me free from any form of bondage and break any form of curses upon my life; this is the day that I will receive a total and complete deliverance in every area of my life, today shall mark the beginning of a new thing in my life.

I am a child of God, born of the Spirit, redeemed by the blood of the Lamb. It is written concerning me that power and authority is given unto me over all devils and to cure diseases, I hereby take authority over any form of curses upon my life, be it ancestral, be it generational, be it demon-inflicted or self-inflicted; I command all curses upon my life to break now by the authority in the name of Jesus Christ. The Bible says, where the word of a king is, there is power; today I speak as a king with the authority and power of the King of kings, and I command every other power to bow in the name of Jesus Christ. I render any power behind any curse upon my life useless and ineffective; I overcome any form of distraction, spiritual laziness and slumber, before the end of this prayer session my testimonies shall manifest without delay by the power in the name of Jesus Christ. Amen!

PRAYER POINTS

1. O God my Father, thank you for being my God, my Father and my friend.
2. O God my Father, thank you for the privilege to know you and the power of the resurrection of Jesus Christ.
3. O God my Father, thank you for always being there for me and with me.

4. O God my Father, thank you for the great and mighty things that you are doing in my life.
5. O God my Father, thank you for your provision and protection over me and my household.
6. O God my Father, thank you for always answering my prayers.
7. I confess my sins before you today and I ask you to forgive me on the basis of your mercy, in the name of Jesus Christ.
8. Wash me clean today O Lord by the blood of Jesus Christ.
9. I cover myself and my household with the blood of Jesus Christ.
10. My prayers today will not go in vain; my prayers will produce the desired results in the name of Jesus Christ.
11. By the power and authority in the blood of Jesus Christ, I bind every spirit of unfruitfulness and I command my barren grounds to be perfectly healed and productive, in the name of Jesus Christ.
12. By the power and authority in the blood of Jesus Christ, I declare that I shall not labor in vain in the name of Jesus Christ.
13. By the power and authority in the blood of Jesus Christ, I declare that the days of my profitless labor are finally over, in the name of Jesus Christ.
14. Every altar of poverty in my foundation working against me; be destroyed now by the fire of God, in the name of Jesus Christ.
15. I stand on the word of God and condemn every mouth speaking lack and poverty into my life, in the name of Jesus Christ.

16. I stand on the word of God and condemn every mouth speaking lack and poverty into my family, in the name of Jesus Christ.
17. I stand on the word of God and condemn every mouth speaking lack and poverty into my marriage, in the name of Jesus Christ.
18. I stand on the word of God and condemn every mouth speaking lack and poverty into the life of my spouse, in the name of Jesus Christ.
19. I stand on the word of God and condemn every mouth speaking lack and poverty into the life of my children, in the name of Jesus Christ.
20. I stand on the word of God and condemn every mouth speaking lack and poverty into my business, in the name of Jesus Christ.
21. I stand on the word of God and condemn every mouth speaking lack and poverty into my finances, in the name of Jesus Christ.
22. Every stronghold of mental poverty in my life; be destroyed now by the fire of God in the name of Jesus Christ.
23. Every stronghold of spiritual poverty in my life; be destroyed now by the fire of God in the name of Jesus Christ.
24. Every stronghold of financial poverty in my life; be destroyed now by the fire of God in the name of Jesus Christ.
25. By the power and authority in the blood of Jesus Christ, I revoke any covenant in my life that is strengthening the stronghold of poverty, in the name of Jesus Christ.

26. By the power and authority in the blood of Jesus Christ, I revoke any covenant in my life that is strengthening the stronghold of lack, in the name of Jesus Christ.
27. By the power and authority in the blood of Jesus Christ, I revoke any covenant in my life that is strengthening the stronghold of almost there, in the name of Jesus Christ.
28. By the power and authority in the blood of Jesus Christ, I revoke any covenant in my life that is strengthening the stronghold of financial failure, in the name of Jesus Christ.
29. By the power and authority in the blood of Jesus Christ, I revoke any covenant in my life that is strengthening the stronghold of financial embarrassment, in the name of Jesus Christ.
30. By the power and authority in the blood of Jesus Christ, I revoke any covenant in my life that is strengthening the stronghold of financial setback, in the name of Jesus Christ.
31. By the power and authority in the blood of Jesus Christ, I revoke any covenant in my life that is strengthening the stronghold of empty pocket, in the name of Jesus Christ.
32. By the power and authority in the blood of Jesus Christ, I revoke any covenant in my life that is strengthening the stronghold of leak-pocket, in the name of Jesus Christ.
33. By the power and authority in the blood of Jesus Christ, I revoke any covenant in my life that is strengthening the stronghold of never had enough, in the name of Jesus Christ.
34. Every stronghold of poverty in my city affecting my finances, I pull you down by the power and authority in the name of Jesus Christ.

35. Every stronghold of poverty in my neighborhood affecting my finances, I pull you down by the power and authority in the name of Jesus Christ.
36. Every stronghold of poverty in my place of work affecting my finances, I pull you down by the power and authority in the name of Jesus Christ.
37. Every stronghold of poverty in the life of my boss affecting my finances, I pull you down by the power and authority in the name of Jesus Christ.
38. Every stronghold of poverty in my family affecting my finances, I pull you down by the power and authority in the name of Jesus Christ.
39. I cancel and neutralize every negative word enforcing poverty into my life, in the name of Jesus Christ.
40. I cancel and neutralize every negative word enforcing poverty into my finances, in the name of Jesus Christ.
41. I cancel and neutralize every negative word enforcing poverty into my marriage, in the name of Jesus Christ.
42. I cancel and neutralize every negative word enforcing poverty into my home, in the name of Jesus Christ.
43. I cancel and neutralize every negative word enforcing poverty into my business, in the name of Jesus Christ.

DAY SEVEN

DELIVERANCE FROM FINANCIAL STRUGGLE

Passages To Read Before You Pray:
Leviticus 26:5, Deuteronomy 8:18, Isaiah 45:1-3, Obadiah 1:17, Psalms 30, 83, Amos 9:13

I stand on the word of God to claim my right as a child of the Kingdom, I cover myself in the blood of Jesus Christ, I cover my household and everything concerning me in the blood of Jesus Christ. I hereby charge this atmosphere by the blood of Jesus Christ and by the fire of the Holy Ghost. I command fresh fire of God to rest upon me now as in the day of Pentecost, let fresh anointing and new oil be released upon me now as I pray. I receive power and authority over the power and the kingdom of darkness, to root out and to pull down, to destroy and to throw down, to build and to plant; whatever I decree in this prayer shall be established; whatever I bind today shall be bound in heaven and whatever I loose today shall be loosed in heaven as it is written in the word of God. Let fresh fire of God be released on my prayer altar and my prayer life now, prince of Persia cannot hinder my prayer, territorial spirit of my neighborhood cannot hinder my prayer, household wickedness cannot hinder my prayer.

I can see my prayer attracting divine intervention. This is the day that the Lord has made, I will rejoice and be glad in it. This is the

day that the Lord has chosen to set me free from any form of bondage and break any form of curses upon my life; this is the day that I will receive a total and complete deliverance in every area of my life, today shall mark the beginning of a new thing in my life.

I am a child of God, born of the Spirit, redeemed by the blood of the Lamb. It is written concerning me that power and authority is given unto me over all devils and to cure diseases, I hereby take authority over any form of curses upon my life, be it ancestral, be it generational, be it demon-inflicted or self-inflicted; I command all curses upon my life to break now by the authority in the name of Jesus Christ. The Bible says, where the word of a king is, there is power; today I speak as a king with the authority and power of the King of kings, and I command every other power to bow in the name of Jesus Christ. I render any power behind any curse upon my life useless and ineffective; I overcome any form of distraction, spiritual laziness and slumber, before the end of this prayer session my testimonies shall manifest without delay by the power in the name of Jesus Christ. Amen!

PRAYER POINTS

1. O God my Father, thank you for being my God, my Father and my friend.
2. O God my Father, thank you for the privilege to know you and the power of the resurrection of Jesus Christ.
3. O God my Father, thank you for always being there for me and with me.

4. O God my Father, thank you for the great and mighty things that you are doing in my life.
5. O God my Father, thank you for your provision and protection over me and my household.
6. O God my Father, thank you for always answering my prayers.
7. I confess my sins before you today and I ask you to forgive me on the basis of your mercy, in the name of Jesus Christ.
8. Wash me clean today O Lord by the blood of Jesus Christ.
9. I cover myself and my household with the blood of Jesus Christ.
10. My prayers today will not go in vain; my prayers will produce the desired results in the name of Jesus Christ.
11. I cut off any connection which my life may have with the curses of poverty by the fire of God, in the name of Jesus Christ.
12. I cut off any connection which my life may have with the curses of poverty from my father's lineage by the fire of God, in the name of Jesus Christ.
13. I cut off any connection which my life may have with the curses of poverty from my mother's lineage by the fire of God, in the name of Jesus Christ.
14. I cut off any connection which my life may have with the curses of financial setback by the fire of God, in the name of Jesus Christ.
15. I cut off any connection which my life may have with the curses of financial setback from my father's lineage by the fire of God, in the name of Jesus Christ.

16. I cut off any connection which my life may have with the curses of financial setback from my mother's lineage by the fire of God, in the name of Jesus Christ.
17. By the power and authority in the blood of Jesus Christ, I command every root of poverty in my life to be destroyed by the fire of God, in the name of Jesus Christ.
18. By the power and authority in the blood of Jesus Christ, I command every root of lack in my life to be destroyed by the fire of God, in the name of Jesus Christ.
19. By the power and authority in the blood of Jesus Christ, I command every root of financial struggle in my life to be destroyed by the fire of God, in the name of Jesus Christ.
20. By the power and authority in the blood of Jesus Christ, I command every root of financial failure in my life to be destroyed by the fire of God, in the name of Jesus Christ.
21. By the power and authority in the blood of Jesus Christ, I command every root of financial setback in my life to be destroyed by the fire of God, in the name of Jesus Christ.
22. By the power and authority in the blood of Jesus Christ, I command every root of financial instability in my life to be destroyed by the fire of God, in the name of Jesus Christ.
23. By the power and authority in the blood of Jesus Christ, I command every root of financial disability in my life to be destroyed by the fire of God, in the name of Jesus Christ.
24. By the power and authority in the blood of Jesus Christ, I command every root of empty pocket in my life to be destroyed by the fire of God, in the name of Jesus Christ.

25. By the power and authority in the blood of Jesus Christ, I command every root of leak-pocket in my life to be destroyed by the fire of God, in the name of Jesus Christ.
26. By the power and authority in the blood of Jesus Christ, I command every root of never had enough in my life to be destroyed by the fire of God, in the name of Jesus Christ.
27. I stand on the word of God and arrest every demonic opposition to my prosperity, I send you down to the pit of hell; you shall come against me no more in the name of Jesus Christ.
28. I stand on the word of God and arrest every demonic opposition to my financial breakthrough, I send you down to the pit of hell; you shall come against me no more in the name of Jesus Christ.
29. I stand on the word of God and arrest every demonic opposition to my financial freedom, I send you down to the pit of hell; you shall come against me no more in the name of Jesus Christ.
30. Today I enter into covenant of wealth and prosperity, in the name of Jesus Christ.
31. As from this moment, I will never lack any good thing again, in the name of Jesus Christ.
32. As from this moment, my portion has changed from beggar to giver, in the name of Jesus Christ.
33. As from this moment, my portion has changed from borrower to lender, in the name of Jesus Christ.
34. Today I command my gates to open so that the wealth of the nations will continually flow into my life, in the name of Jesus Christ.
35. O God my Father, endow me with the required mental skills to interpret every opportunity that comes my way

correctly and take maximum advantage of them, in the name of Jesus Christ.
36. O God my Father, let the anointing for money yielding-ideas fall upon me now, in the name of Jesus Christ.
37. O God my Father, let people of all tribes, languages, and nations come together to bless me, in the name of Jesus Christ.
38. O God my Father, visit my house today and turn my water into your best wine, in the name of Jesus Christ.
39. O God my Father, manifest your power in my life today and let poverty in my life turn miraculously to prosperity, in the name of Jesus Christ.
40. O God my Father, manifest your power in my life today and let lack in my life turn miraculously to abundance, in the name of Jesus Christ.
41. O God my Father, manifest your power in my life today and let never had enough in my life turn miraculously to surplus, in the name of Jesus Christ.
42. O God my Father, anoint my head today with oil of prosperity and let my bank accounts overflow with money, in the name of Jesus Christ.
43. Abundance is your nature, O God my Father, demonstrate this aspect of yourself in my life, in the name of Jesus Christ.
44. O God my Father, take what is ordinary and common in my life and make it extraordinary, the very richest and most choice life anyone can ever imagine, in the name of Jesus Christ.
45. O God my Father, manifest your power in my life and transform my finances, in the name of Jesus Christ.

DELIVERANCE FROM ANCESTRAL CURSES OF REJECTION

(7 DAYS FASTING & INTENSIVE PRAYER)

KEY BIBLE PASSAGE

"Behold, the days come, saith the LORD, that I will sow the house of Israel and the house of Judah with the seed of man, and with the seed of beast. And it shall come to pass, that like as I have watched over them, to pluck up, and to break down, and to throw down, and to destroy, and to afflict; so will I watch over them, to build, and to plant, saith the LORD.

In those days they shall say no more, The fathers have eaten a sour grape, and the children's teeth are set on edge. But every one shall die for his own iniquity: every man that eateth the sour grape, his teeth shall be set on edge.

Behold, the days come, saith the LORD, that I will make a new covenant with the house of Israel, and with the house of Judah: Not according to the covenant that I made with their fathers in the day that I took them by the hand to bring them out of the land of Egypt; which my covenant they brake, although I was an husband unto them, saith the LORD." – Jeremiah 31:27-32

DAY ONE

GENERATIONAL REPENTANCE

Passages To Read Before You Pray:
Exodus 20:1-5, Jeremiah 31:27-34, Daniel 9:1-19, Psalms 89

I stand on the word of God to claim my right as a child of the Kingdom, I cover myself in the blood of Jesus Christ, I cover my household and everything concerning me in the blood of Jesus Christ. I hereby charge this atmosphere by the blood of Jesus Christ and by the fire of the Holy Ghost. I command fresh fire of God to rest upon me now as in the day of Pentecost, let fresh anointing and new oil be released upon me now as I pray. I receive power and authority over the power and the kingdom of darkness, to root out and to pull down, to destroy and to throw down, to build and to plant; whatever I decree in this prayer shall be established; whatever I bind today shall be bound in heaven and whatever I loose today shall be loosed in heaven as it is written in the word of God. Let fresh fire of God be released on my prayer altar and my prayer life now, prince of Persia cannot hinder my prayer, territorial spirit of my neighborhood cannot hinder my prayer, household wickedness cannot hinder my prayer.

I can see my prayer attracting divine intervention. This is the day that the Lord has made, I will rejoice and be glad in it. This is the day that the Lord has chosen to set me free from any form of

bondage and break any form of curses upon my life; this is the day that I will receive a total and complete deliverance in every area of my life, today shall mark the beginning of a new thing in my life.

I am a child of God, born of the Spirit, redeemed by the blood of the Lamb. It is written concerning me that power and authority is given unto me over all devils and to cure diseases, I hereby take authority over any form of curses upon my life, be it ancestral, be it generational, be it demon-inflicted or self-inflicted; I command all curses upon my life to break now by the authority in the name of Jesus Christ. The Bible says, where the word of a king is, there is power; today I speak as a king with the authority and power of the King of kings, and I command every other power to bow in the name of Jesus Christ. I render any power behind any curse upon my life useless and ineffective; I overcome any form of distraction, spiritual laziness and slumber, before the end of this prayer session my testimonies shall manifest without delay by the power in the name of Jesus Christ. Amen!

PRAYER POINTS

1. O God my Father, thank you for being my God, my Father and my friend.
2. O God my Father, thank you for the privilege to know you and the power of the resurrection of Jesus Christ.
3. O God my Father, thank you for always being there for me and with me.
4. O God my Father, thank you for the great and mighty things that you are doing in my life.

5. O God my Father, thank you for your provision and protection over me and my household.
6. O God my Father, thank you for always answering my prayers.
7. O God my Father, I confess and repent of all sins in my life or my ancestors' lives that have resulted in a curse upon my life or bloodline; forgive me Lord on the basis of your mercy and cleanse me by the blood of Jesus Christ.
8. O God my Father, I confess today and repent of all sins of disobedience in my life or my ancestor's lives that have resulted in a curse upon my life or bloodline; forgive me Lord on the basis of your mercy and cleanse me by the blood of Jesus Christ.
9. O God my Father, I confess today and repent of all sins of rebellion in my life or my ancestor's lives that have resulted in a curse upon my life or bloodline; forgive me Lord on the basis of your mercy and cleanse me by the blood of Jesus Christ.
10. O God my Father, I confess today and repent of all sins of perversion in my life or my ancestor's lives that have resulted in a curse upon my life or bloodline; forgive me Lord on the basis of your mercy and cleanse me by the blood of Jesus Christ.
11. O God my Father, I confess today and repent of all sins of witchcraft in my life or my ancestor's lives that have resulted in a curse upon my life or bloodline; forgive me Lord on the basis of your mercy and cleanse me by the blood of Jesus Christ.
12. O God my Father, I confess today and repent of all sins of idolatry in my life or my ancestor's lives that have resulted in a curse upon my life or bloodline; forgive me

Lord on the basis of your mercy and cleanse me by the blood of Jesus Christ.
13. O God my Father, I confess today and repent of all sins of lust in my life or my ancestor's lives that have resulted in a curse upon my life or bloodline; forgive me Lord on the basis of your mercy and cleanse me by the blood of Jesus Christ.
14. O God my Father, I confess today and repent of all sins of adultery in my life or my ancestor's lives that have resulted in a curse upon my life or bloodline; forgive me Lord on the basis of your mercy and cleanse me by the blood of Jesus Christ.
15. O God my Father, I confess today and repent of all sins of fornication in my life or my ancestor's lives that have resulted in a curse upon my life or bloodline; forgive me Lord on the basis of your mercy and cleanse me by the blood of Jesus Christ.
16. O God my Father, I confess today and repent of all sins of mistreatment of others in my life or my ancestor's lives that have resulted in a curse upon my life or bloodline; forgive me Lord on the basis of your mercy and cleanse me by the blood of Jesus Christ.
17. O God my Father, I confess today and repent of all sins of murder or abortion in my life or my ancestor's lives that have resulted in a curse upon my life or bloodline; forgive me Lord on the basis of your mercy and cleanse me by the blood of Jesus Christ.
18. O God my Father, I confess today and repent of all sins of cheating in my life or my ancestor's lives that have resulted in a curse upon my life or bloodline; forgive me Lord on the basis of your mercy and cleanse me by the blood of Jesus Christ.

19. O God my Father, I confess today and repent of all sins of lying in my life or my ancestor's lives that have resulted in a curse upon my life or bloodline; forgive me Lord on the basis of your mercy and cleanse me by the blood of Jesus Christ.
20. O God my Father, I confess today and repent of all sins of sorcery in my life or my ancestor's lives that have resulted in a curse upon my life or bloodline; forgive me Lord on the basis of your mercy and cleanse me by the blood of Jesus Christ.
21. O God my Father, I confess today and repent of all sins of divination in my life or my ancestor's lives that have resulted in a curse upon my life or bloodline; forgive me Lord on the basis of your mercy and cleanse me by the blood of Jesus Christ.
22. O God my Father, I confess today and repent of all sins of occult involvement in my life or my ancestor's lives that have resulted in a curse upon my life or bloodline; forgive me Lord on the basis of your mercy and cleanse me by the blood of Jesus Christ.
23. I disassociate myself from all evil done by my ancestors by the power in the blood of Jesus Christ.
24. I disassociate myself from all evil attitudes done by my ancestors against the will and purpose of God, in the name of Jesus Christ.
25. With all my heart I disagree with all sins committed by my ancestors, Father Lord have mercy and cleanse me by the blood of Jesus Christ.
26. Today with all my heart I declare that I refuse to be like my parents, in the name of Jesus Christ.
27. Today with all my heart I declare that I refuse to be like any of my ancestors, in the name of Jesus Christ.

28. I refuse to suffer the same problems as my parents, I reject it; my heart, soul, spirit and body reject it in the name of Jesus Christ.
29. I refuse to suffer the same problems as any of my ancestors, I reject it; my heart, soul, spirit and body reject it in the name of Jesus Christ.
30. In the name of Jesus Christ, I refuse to go through what my parents went through, my case is different, I am a child of God and covered by the blood of Jesus Christ.
31. By the power and authority in the blood of Jesus Christ, I severe myself from my bloodline, in the name of Jesus Christ.
32. By the power and authority in the blood of Jesus Christ, I severe myself from the connection to any of my ancestors, in the name of Jesus Christ.
33. By the power and authority in the blood of Jesus Christ, I severe myself from spiritual connection to any of my ancestors, in the name of Jesus Christ.
34. By the power and authority in the blood of Jesus Christ, I severe myself from physical connection to any of my ancestors, in the name of Jesus Christ.
35. By the power and authority in the blood of Jesus Christ, I severe myself from emotional connection to any of my ancestors, in the name of Jesus Christ.
36. By the power and authority in the blood of Jesus Christ, I severe myself from mental connection to any of my ancestors, in the name of Jesus Christ.
37. By the power and authority in the blood of Jesus Christ, I severe myself from the connection to the idol of my father's house, in the name of Jesus Christ.

38. By the power and authority in the blood of Jesus Christ, I sever myself from the connection to the idol of my mother's house, in the name of Jesus Christ.
39. By the power and authority in the blood of Jesus Christ, I destroy every spiritual DNA that links me to my ancestors by the fire of God, in the name of Jesus Christ.
40. By the power and authority in the blood of Jesus Christ, I destroy every spiritual DNA that links my children to my ancestors by the fire of God, in the name of Jesus Christ.

DAY TWO

DELIVERANCE FROM SATANIC ATTACKS

Passages To Read Before You Pray:
Ephesians 6:10-18, Jeremiah 1:8, 19, Isaiah 50:7-9, Psalms 55, 35, Galatians 3:13, Isaiah 10:27

I stand on the word of God to claim my right as a child of the Kingdom, I cover myself in the blood of Jesus Christ, I cover my household and everything concerning me in the blood of Jesus Christ. I hereby charge this atmosphere by the blood of Jesus Christ and by the fire of the Holy Ghost. I command fresh fire of God to rest upon me now as in the day of Pentecost, let fresh anointing and new oil be released upon me now as I pray. I receive power and authority over the power and the kingdom of darkness, to root out and to pull down, to destroy and to throw down, to build and to plant; whatever I decree in this prayer shall be established; whatever I bind today shall be bound in heaven and whatever I loose today shall be loosed in heaven as it is written in the word of God. Let fresh fire of God be released on my prayer altar and my prayer life now, prince of Persia cannot hinder my prayer, territorial spirit of my neighborhood cannot hinder my prayer, household wickedness cannot hinder my prayer.

I can see my prayer attracting divine intervention. This is the day that the Lord has made, I will rejoice and be glad in it. This is the

day that the Lord has chosen to set me free from any form of bondage and break any form of curses upon my life; this is the day that I will receive a total and complete deliverance in every area of my life, today shall mark the beginning of a new thing in my life.

I am a child of God, born of the Spirit, redeemed by the blood of the Lamb. It is written concerning me that power and authority is given unto me over all devils and to cure diseases, I hereby take authority over any form of curses upon my life, be it ancestral, be it generational, be it demon-inflicted or self-inflicted; I command all curses upon my life to break now by the authority in the name of Jesus Christ. The Bible says, where the word of a king is, there is power; today I speak as a king with the authority and power of the King of kings, and I command every other power to bow in the name of Jesus Christ. I render any power behind any curse upon my life useless and ineffective; I overcome any form of distraction, spiritual laziness and slumber, before the end of this prayer session my testimonies shall manifest without delay by the power in the name of Jesus Christ. Amen!

PRAYER POINTS

1. God my Father, thank you for being my God, my Father and my friend.
2. God my Father, thank you for the privilege to know you and the power of the resurrection of Jesus Christ.
3. God my Father, thank you for always being there for me and with me.

4. God my Father, thank you for the great and mighty things that you are doing in my life.
5. God my Father, thank you for your provision and protection over me and my household.
6. God my Father, thank you for always answering my prayers.
7. I confess my sins before you today and I ask you to forgive me on the basis of your mercy, in the name of Jesus Christ.
8. Wash me clean today O Lord by the blood of Jesus Christ.
9. I cover myself and my household with the blood of Jesus Christ.
10. My prayers today will not go in vain; my prayers will produce the desired results in the name of Jesus Christ.
11. By the power and authority in the blood of Jesus Christ, I command every curse of rejection upon my life to break now, in the name of Jesus Christ.
12. By the power and authority in the blood of Jesus Christ, I am delivered today from every work of darkness, in the name of Jesus Christ.
13. By the power and authority in the blood of Jesus Christ, today I decree deliverance from every assignment of darkness against my life, in the name of Jesus Christ.
14. By the power and authority in the blood of Jesus Christ, today I decree deliverance from every assignment of darkness against my family, in the name of Jesus Christ.
15. By the power and authority in the blood of Jesus Christ, today I decree deliverance from every assignment of darkness against my spouse, in the name of Jesus Christ.

16. By the power and authority in the blood of Jesus Christ, today I decree deliverance from every assignment of darkness against my children, in the name of Jesus Christ.
17. By the power and authority in the blood of Jesus Christ, today I decree deliverance from every assignment of darkness against my marriage, in the name of Jesus Christ.
18. By the power and authority in the blood of Jesus Christ, today I decree deliverance from every assignment of darkness against my finances, in the name of Jesus Christ.
19. By the power and authority in the blood of Jesus Christ, today I decree deliverance from every assignment of darkness against my business, in the name of Jesus Christ.
20. By the power and authority in the blood of Jesus Christ, today I decree deliverance from every assignment of darkness against my destiny, in the name of Jesus Christ.
21. By the power and authority in the blood of Jesus Christ, today I decree deliverance from every curse of rejection, in the name of Jesus Christ.
22. By the power and authority in the name of Jesus Christ, today I decree deliverance from the words of darkness spoken into my life, in the name of Jesus Christ.
23. By the power and authority in the name of Jesus Christ, today I decree deliverance from the words of darkness spoken into my family, in the name of Jesus Christ.
24. By the power and authority in the name of Jesus Christ, today I decree deliverance from the words of darkness spoken into my marriage, in the name of Jesus Christ.

25. By the power and authority in the name of Jesus Christ, today I decree deliverance from the words of darkness spoken into the life of my spouse, in the name of Jesus Christ.
26. By the power and authority in the name of Jesus Christ, today I decree deliverance from the words of darkness spoken into the lives of my children, in the name of Jesus Christ.
27. By the power and authority in the name of Jesus Christ, today I decree deliverance from the words of darkness spoken into my business, in the name of Jesus Christ.
28. By the power and authority in the name of Jesus Christ, today I decree deliverance from the words of darkness spoken into my finances, in the name of Jesus Christ.
29. By the power and authority in the name of Jesus Christ today I decree deliverance from the words of darkness spoken against the works of my hands, in the name of Jesus Christ.
30. By the power and authority in the blood of Jesus Christ, I am delivered today from every companion spirit of rejection, in the name of Jesus Christ.
31. By the power and authority in the blood of Jesus Christ, I am delivered today from the effects of the spirit of abandonment, in the name of Jesus Christ.
32. By the power and authority in the blood of Jesus Christ, I am delivered today from the spirit of non-acceptance in the name of Jesus Christ.
33. I come against you spirit of rejection, you cannot control my life, I bind and cast you out of my life right now, in the name of Jesus Christ.

34. I come against you spirit of rejection, you cannot control my marital life, I bind and cast you out of my life right now, in the name of Jesus Christ.
35. I come against you spirit of rejection, you cannot control my level of success, I bind and cast you out of my life right now, in the name of Jesus Christ.
36. I come against you spirit of rejection, you cannot control my destiny, I bind and cast you out of my life right now, in the name of Jesus Christ.
37. I come against you spirit of rejection, you cannot control my life's progress, I bind and cast you out of my life right now, in the name of Jesus Christ.

DAY THREE

DELIVERANCE FROM ANCESTRAL CURSES OF REJECTION

Passages To Read Before You Pray:
Isaiah 54:1-17, Jeremiah 31:27-32, Psalms 59, 69, 66, 70, 86, 140, 24

I stand on the word of God to claim my right as a child of the Kingdom, I cover myself in the blood of Jesus Christ, I cover my household and everything concerning me in the blood of Jesus Christ. I hereby charge this atmosphere by the blood of Jesus Christ and by the fire of the Holy Ghost. I command fresh fire of God to rest upon me now as in the day of Pentecost, let fresh anointing and new oil be released upon me now as I pray. I receive power and authority over the power and the kingdom of darkness, to root out and to pull down, to destroy and to throw down, to build and to plant; whatever I decree in this prayer shall be established; whatever I bind today shall be bound in heaven and whatever I loose today shall be loosed in heaven as it is written in the word of God. Let fresh fire of God be released on my prayer altar and my prayer life now, prince of Persia cannot hinder my prayer, territorial spirit of my neighborhood cannot hinder my prayer, household wickedness cannot hinder my prayer.

I can see my prayer attracting divine intervention. This is the day that the Lord has made, I will rejoice and be glad in it. This is the day that the Lord has chosen to set me free from any form of bondage and break any form of curses upon my life; this is the day that I will receive a total and complete deliverance in every area of my life, today shall mark the beginning of a new thing in my life.

I am a child of God, born of the Spirit, redeemed by the blood of the Lamb. It is written concerning me that power and authority is given unto me over all devils and to cure diseases, I hereby take authority over any form of curses upon my life, be it ancestral, be it generational, be it demon-inflicted or self-inflicted; I command all curses upon my life to break now by the authority in the name of Jesus Christ. The Bible says, where the word of a king is, there is power; today I speak as a king with the authority and power of the King of kings, and I command every other power to bow in the name of Jesus Christ. I render any power behind any curse upon my life useless and ineffective; I overcome any form of distraction, spiritual laziness and slumber, before the end of this prayer session my testimonies shall manifest without delay by the power in the name of Jesus Christ. Amen!

PRAYER POINTS

1. O God my Father, thank you for being my God, my Father and my friend.
2. O God my Father, thank you for the privilege to know you and the power of the resurrection of Jesus Christ.

3. O God my Father, thank you for always being there for me and with me.
4. O God my Father, thank you for the great and mighty things that you are doing in my life.
5. O God my Father, thank you for your provision and protection over me and my household.
6. O God my Father, thank you for always answering my prayers.
7. I confess my sins before you today and I ask you to forgive me on the basis of your mercy, in the name of Jesus Christ.
8. Wash me clean today O Lord by the blood of Jesus Christ.
9. I cover myself and my household with the blood of Jesus Christ.
10. My prayers today will not go in vain; my prayers will produce the desired results in the name of Jesus Christ.
11. I come against you spirit of rejection, you cannot control my family, I bind and cast you out of my life right now, in the name of Jesus Christ.
12. Curses of rejection that has been affecting my family line since the time of Adam the first man to me, I command you to break now by the power and authority in the name of Jesus Christ. You will no longer affect me.
13. Curses of rejection that has been affecting my family line since the time of Adam the first man to me, I command you to break now by the power and authority in the name of Jesus Christ. You will no longer affect my marriage.
14. Curses of rejection that has been affecting my family line since the time of Adam the first man to me, I

command you to break now by the power and authority in the name of Jesus Christ. You will no longer affect my family.

15. Curses of rejection that has been affecting my family line since the time of Adam the first man to me, I command you to break now by the power and authority in the name of Jesus Christ. You will no longer affect my spouse.
16. Curses of rejection that has been affecting my family line since the time of Adam the first man to me, I command you to break now by the power and authority in the name of Jesus Christ. You will no longer affect my children.
17. Curses of rejection that has been affecting my family line since the time of Adam the first man to me, I command you to break now by the power and authority in the name of Jesus Christ. You will no longer affect my level of success.
18. Curses of rejection that has been affecting my family line since the time of Adam the first man to me, I command you to break now by the power and authority in the name of Jesus Christ. You will no longer affect my business.
19. Curses of rejection causing me to be rejected when I am looking for jobs, enough is enough, I command you to break now by the power and authority in the name of Jesus Christ.
20. Curses of rejection causing me to be rejected by the people that I know, enough is enough, I command you to break now by the power and authority in the name of Jesus Christ.

21. Curses of rejection causing me to be rejected by the people that I don't know, enough is enough, I command you to break now by the power and authority in the name of Jesus Christ.
22. Curses of rejection causing me to be rejected by my friends, enough is enough, I command you to break now by the power and authority in the name of Jesus Christ.
23. Curses of rejection causing me to be rejected by my family, enough is enough, I command you to break now by the power and authority in the name of Jesus Christ.
24. Curses of rejection causing me to be rejected in the community, enough is enough, I command you to break now by the power and authority in the name of Jesus Christ.
25. Curses of rejection causing my applications to be rejected, enough is enough, I command you to break now by the power and authority in the name of Jesus Christ.
26. Curses of rejection causing my plans to be rejected, enough is enough, I command you to break now by the power and authority in the name of Jesus Christ.
27. Curses of rejection causing my ideas to be rejected, enough is enough, I command you to break now by the power and authority in the name of Jesus Christ.
28. Curses of rejection causing me to lose my divine opportunities, enough is enough, I command you to break now by the power and authority in the name of Jesus Christ.
29. Every evil covenant that is directly responsible for curses of rejection upon my life; be revoked now by the power and authority in the blood of Jesus Christ.

30. Every evil covenant that is directly responsible for curses of rejection upon my family; be revoked now by the power and authority in the blood of Jesus Christ.
31. Every evil covenant that is directly responsible for curses of rejection upon my spouse; be revoked now by the power and authority in the blood of Jesus Christ.
32. Every evil covenant that is directly responsible for curses of rejection upon my children; be revoked now by the power and authority in the blood of Jesus Christ.
33. Household wickedness that is directly responsible for curses of rejection upon my life; you will not escape the judgment of God, in the name of Jesus Christ.
34. Witchcraft power that is directly responsible for curses of rejection upon my life; you will not escape the judgment of God, in the name of Jesus Christ.
35. Satanic agent that is directly responsible for curses of rejection upon my life; you will not escape the judgment of God, in the name of Jesus Christ.
36. By the power and authority in the blood of Jesus Christ, I bind inherited curses of rejection and cast it out of my life right now by the power in the name of Jesus Christ.
37. You spirit of rejection programmed into my genes, I command you to come out now and never come back in the name of Jesus Christ.
38. You spirit of rejection programmed into my bloodline, I command you to come out now and never come back in the name of Jesus Christ.
39. You spirit of rejection programmed into the lives of my children, I command you to come out now and never come back in the name of Jesus Christ.

40. You spirit of rejection programmed into the life of my spouse, I command you to come out now and never come back in the name of Jesus Christ.
41. You spirit of hatred programmed into my genes, I command you to come out now and never come back in the name of Jesus Christ.
42. You spirit of hatred programmed into my bloodline, I command you to come out now and never come back in the name of Jesus Christ.
43. You spirit of hatred programmed into the lives of my children, I command you to come out now and never come back in the name of Jesus Christ.
44. You spirit of hatred programmed into the life of my spouse, I command you to come out now and never come back in the name of Jesus Christ.

DAY FOUR

PRAYER TO ERASE MARKS OF REJECTION

Passages To Read Before You Pray:
Revelation 12:11, Colossians 2:13-15, Psalms 9, 19, 42, 35, 70, 140, 83

I stand on the word of God to claim my right as a child of the Kingdom, I cover myself in the blood of Jesus Christ, I cover my household and everything concerning me in the blood of Jesus Christ. I hereby charge this atmosphere by the blood of Jesus Christ and by the fire of the Holy Ghost. I command fresh fire of God to rest upon me now as in the day of Pentecost, let fresh anointing and new oil be released upon me now as I pray. I receive power and authority over the power and the kingdom of darkness, to root out and to pull down, to destroy and to throw down, to build and to plant; whatever I decree in this prayer shall be established; whatever I bind today shall be bound in heaven and whatever I loose today shall be loosed in heaven as it is written in the word of God. Let fresh fire of God be released on my prayer altar and my prayer life now, prince of Persia cannot hinder my prayer, territorial spirit of my neighborhood cannot hinder my prayer, household wickedness cannot hinder my prayer.

I can see my prayer attracting divine intervention. This is the day that the Lord has made, I will rejoice and be glad in it. This is the

day that the Lord has chosen to set me free from any form of bondage and break any form of curses upon my life; this is the day that I will receive a total and complete deliverance in every area of my life, today shall mark the beginning of a new thing in my life.

I am a child of God, born of the Spirit, redeemed by the blood of the Lamb. It is written concerning me that power and authority is given unto me over all devils and to cure diseases, I hereby take authority over any form of curses upon my life, be it ancestral, be it generational, be it demon-inflicted or self-inflicted; I command all curses upon my life to break now by the authority in the name of Jesus Christ. The Bible says, where the word of a king is, there is power; today I speak as a king with the authority and power of the King of kings, and I command every other power to bow in the name of Jesus Christ. I render any power behind any curse upon my life useless and ineffective; I overcome any form of distraction, spiritual laziness and slumber, before the end of this prayer session my testimonies shall manifest without delay by the power in the name of Jesus Christ. Amen!

PRAYER POINTS

1. O God my Father, thank you for being my God, my Father and my friend.
2. O God my Father, thank you for the privilege to know you and the power of the resurrection of Jesus Christ.
3. O God my Father, thank you for always being there for me and with me.

4. O God my Father, thank you for the great and mighty things that you are doing in my life.
5. O God my Father, thank you for your provision and protection over me and my household.
6. O God my Father, thank you for always answering my prayers.
7. I confess my sins before you today and I ask you to forgive me on the basis of your mercy, in the name of Jesus Christ.
8. Wash me clean today O Lord by the blood of Jesus Christ.
9. I cover myself and my household with the blood of Jesus Christ.
10. My prayers today will not go in vain; my prayers will produce the desired results in the name of Jesus Christ.
11. I take authority over every spirit of rejection working against me, I command you to release me now and let me go, in the name of Jesus Christ.
12. I take authority over every spirit of rejection that has been working against my family line, I command you to release us now and let us go, in the name of Jesus Christ.
13. I take authority over every spirit of rejection working against my spouse, I command you to release my spouse now and let him/her go, in the name of Jesus Christ.
14. I take authority over every spirit of rejection working against my children, I command you to release them now and let them go, in the name of Jesus Christ.
15. Every dream of rejection I have ever had, I cancel you today by the power in the blood of Jesus Christ.
16. Every evil mark of rejection upon my life; be erased now by the blood of Jesus Christ.

17. Every evil mark of rejection upon my family; be erased now by the blood of Jesus Christ.
18. Every evil mark of rejection upon my marriage; be erased now by the blood of Jesus Christ.
19. Every evil mark of rejection upon my spouse; be erased now by the blood of Jesus Christ.
20. Every evil mark of rejection upon my children; be erased now by the blood of Jesus Christ.
21. Every evil mark of rejection upon my application; be erased now by the blood of Jesus Christ.
22. Every evil mark of rejection upon my resume; be erased now by the blood of Jesus Christ.
23. Every evil mark of rejection upon my business plan; be erased now by the blood of Jesus Christ.
24. Every evil mark of rejection upon every area of my interest; be erased now by the blood of Jesus Christ.
25. Inherited curses of rejection attached to my life, I break you off today by the power in the name of Jesus Christ.
26. Inherited curses of rejection attached to my destiny, I break you off today by the power in the name of Jesus Christ.
27. Inherited curses of rejection attached to my family, I break you off today by the power in the name of Jesus Christ.
28. Inherited curses of rejection attached to my business, I break you off today by the power in the name of Jesus Christ.
29. Generational curses of rejection, enough is enough, come out of my life now in the name of Jesus Christ.
30. Generational curses of rejection, enough is enough, come out of my family now, in the name of Jesus Christ.

31. Foundational curses of rejection, loose your hold over my life right now, in the name of Jesus Christ.
32. Foundational curses of rejection, loose your hold over my family right now, in the name of Jesus Christ.
33. Foundational curses of rejection, loose your hold over my marriage right now, in the name of Jesus Christ.
34. Foundational curses of rejection, loose your hold over my children right now, in the name of Jesus Christ.
35. Foundational curses of rejection, loose your hold over my spouse right now, in the name of Jesus Christ.
36. Foundational curses of rejection, loose your hold over my business right now, in the name of Jesus Christ.
37. Foundational curses of rejection, loose your hold over my finances right now, in the name of Jesus Christ.
38. Foundational curses of rejection, loose your hold over my destiny right now, in the name of Jesus Christ.

DAY FIVE

PRAYER TO OVERCOME FEAR OF REJECTION

Passages To Read Before You Pray:
Isaiah 41:10-13, Revelation 12:11, Psalms 23, 27, 40, 106, 107

I stand on the word of God to claim my right as a child of the Kingdom, I cover myself in the blood of Jesus Christ, I cover my household and everything concerning me in the blood of Jesus Christ. I hereby charge this atmosphere by the blood of Jesus Christ and by the fire of the Holy Ghost. I command fresh fire of God to rest upon me now as in the day of Pentecost, let fresh anointing and new oil be released upon me now as I pray. I receive power and authority over the power and the kingdom of darkness, to root out and to pull down, to destroy and to throw down, to build and to plant; whatever I decree in this prayer shall be established; whatever I bind today shall be bound in heaven and whatever I loose today shall be loosed in heaven as it is written in the word of God. Let fresh fire of God be released on my prayer altar and my prayer life now, prince of Persia cannot hinder my prayer, territorial spirit of my neighborhood cannot hinder my prayer, household wickedness cannot hinder my prayer.

I can see my prayer attracting divine intervention. This is the day that the Lord has made, I will rejoice and be glad in it. This is the day that the Lord has chosen to set me free from any form of

bondage and break any form of curses upon my life; this is the day that I will receive a total and complete deliverance in every area of my life, today shall mark the beginning of a new thing in my life.

I am a child of God, born of the Spirit, redeemed by the blood of the Lamb. It is written concerning me that power and authority is given unto me over all devils and to cure diseases, I hereby take authority over any form of curses upon my life, be it ancestral, be it generational, be it demon-inflicted or self-inflicted; I command all curses upon my life to break now by the authority in the name of Jesus Christ. The Bible says, where the word of a king is, there is power; today I speak as a king with the authority and power of the King of kings, and I command every other power to bow in the name of Jesus Christ. I render any power behind any curse upon my life useless and ineffective; I overcome any form of distraction, spiritual laziness and slumber, before the end of this prayer session my testimonies shall manifest without delay by the power in the name of Jesus Christ. Amen!

PRAYER POINTS

1. O God my Father, thank you for being my God, my Father and my friend.
2. O God my Father, thank you for the privilege to know you and the power of the resurrection of Jesus Christ.
3. O God my Father, thank you for always being there for me and with me.
4. O God my Father, thank you for the great and mighty things that you are doing in my life.

5. O God my Father, thank you for your provision and protection over me and my household.
6. O God my Father, thank you for always answering my prayers.
7. I confess my sins before you today and I ask you to forgive me on the basis of your mercy, in the name of Jesus Christ.
8. Wash me clean today O Lord by the blood of Jesus Christ.
9. I cover myself and my household with the blood of Jesus Christ.
10. My prayers today will not go in vain; my prayers will produce the desired results in the name of Jesus Christ.
11. Every curse of rejection running in my family line that has overshadowed my blessings, I command you to break now by the authority in the name of Jesus Christ.
12. Every curse of rejection running in my family line that has overshadowed my breakthroughs, I command you to break now by the authority in the name of Jesus Christ.
13. Every curse of rejection running in my family line that has overshadowed my financial freedom, I command you to break now by the authority in the name of Jesus Christ.
14. Every curse of rejection running in my family line that has overshadowed my divine opportunities, I command you to break now by the authority in the name of Jesus Christ.
15. Every curse of rejection running in my family line that has overshadowed my progress, I command you to break now by the authority in the name of Jesus Christ.

16. By the power and authority in the blood of Jesus Christ, I come out of every satanic prison in the name of Jesus Christ.
17. Today I renounce the inherited curses of rejection that has been passed down to me by my ancestors, in the name of Jesus Christ.
18. Today I renounce the spirits of fear of rejection that may have entered my life through unbelief, in the name of Jesus Christ.
19. Today I renounce the spirits of fear of rejection that may have entered my life one way or the other, in the name of Jesus Christ.
20. Today I renounce the spirits of self-rejection that may have entered my life through unbelief, in the name of Jesus Christ.
21. Today I renounce the spirits of self-rejection that may have entered my life one way or the other, in the name of Jesus Christ.
22. Today I renounce the spirits of perceived rejection that may have entered my life one way or the other, in the name of Jesus Christ.
23. You spirit of rejection, your legal right to operate in my life has been taken away on the cross of Calvary; you must leave now and never come back in the name of Jesus Christ.
24. You spirit of rejection, your legal right to operate in the life of my spouse has been taken away on the cross of Calvary; you must leave now and never come back in the name of Jesus Christ.
25. You spirit of rejection, your legal right to operate in the lives of children has been taken away on the cross of

Calvary; you must leave now and never come back in the name of Jesus Christ.

26. You spirit of rejection, your legal right to operate in my family has been taken away on the cross of Calvary; you must leave now and never come back in the name of Jesus Christ.

27. You spirit of rejection, your legal right to operate in my marriage has been taken away on the cross of Calvary; you must leave now and never come back in the name of Jesus Christ.

28. You spirit of rejection, your legal right to operate in my business has been taken away on the cross of Calvary; you must leave now and never come back in the name of Jesus Christ.

29. Spirit of rejection, I bind and cast you out of my life now in the name of Jesus Christ; and I forbid you to ever operate in my life again.

30. Spirit of rejection, I bind and cast you out of my family now in the name of Jesus Christ; and I forbid you to ever operate in my family again.

31. Spirit of rejection, I bind and cast you out of my business now in the name of Jesus Christ; and I forbid you to ever operate in my business again.

32. Spirit of rejection, I bind and cast you out of my finances now in the name of Jesus Christ; and I forbid you to ever operate in my finances again.

33. Today I nullify every word of rejection spoken against me when I was in my mother's womb, in the name of Jesus Christ.

34. Today I nullify every word of rejection spoken against me when my parents discovered my gender at birth, in the name of Jesus Christ.

35. Today I nullify every word of rejection spoken against me when I was growing up, in the name of Jesus Christ.

DAY SIX

DELIVERANCE FROM FOUNDATIONAL REJECTION

Passages To Read Before You Pray:
2 Kings 2:19-22, 2 Corinthians 10:3-6, Exodus 14:13-14, 2 Chronicles 7:14, Psalms 29, 42, 3, 9, 140

I stand on the word of God to claim my right as a child of the Kingdom, I cover myself in the blood of Jesus Christ, I cover my household and everything concerning me in the blood of Jesus Christ. I hereby charge this atmosphere by the blood of Jesus Christ and by the fire of the Holy Ghost. I command fresh fire of God to rest upon me now as in the day of Pentecost, let fresh anointing and new oil be released upon me now as I pray. I receive power and authority over the power and the kingdom of darkness, to root out and to pull down, to destroy and to throw down, to build and to plant; whatever I decree in this prayer shall be established; whatever I bind today shall be bound in heaven and whatever I loose today shall be loosed in heaven as it is written in the word of God. Let fresh fire of God be released on my prayer altar and my prayer life now, prince of Persia cannot hinder my prayer, territorial spirit of my neighborhood cannot hinder my prayer, household wickedness cannot hinder my prayer.

I can see my prayer attracting divine intervention. This is the day that the Lord has made, I will rejoice and be glad in it. This is the

day that the Lord has chosen to set me free from any form of bondage and break any form of curses upon my life; this is the day that I will receive a total and complete deliverance in every area of my life, today shall mark the beginning of a new thing in my life.

I am a child of God, born of the Spirit, redeemed by the blood of the Lamb. It is written concerning me that power and authority is given unto me over all devils and to cure diseases, I hereby take authority over any form of curses upon my life, be it ancestral, be it generational, be it demon-inflicted or self-inflicted; I command all curses upon my life to break now by the authority in the name of Jesus Christ. The Bible says, where the word of a king is, there is power; today I speak as a king with the authority and power of the King of kings, and I command every other power to bow in the name of Jesus Christ. I render any power behind any curse upon my life useless and ineffective; I overcome any form of distraction, spiritual laziness and slumber, before the end of this prayer session my testimonies shall manifest without delay by the power in the name of Jesus Christ. Amen!

PRAYER POINTS

1. O God my Father, thank you for being my God, my Father and my friend.
2. O God my Father, thank you for the privilege to know you and the power of the resurrection of Jesus Christ.
3. O God my Father, thank you for always being there for me and with me.

4. O God my Father, thank you for the great and mighty things that you are doing in my life.
5. O God my Father, thank you for your provision and protection over me and my household.
6. O God my Father, thank you for always answering my prayers.
7. I confess my sins before you today and I ask you to forgive me on the basis of your mercy, in the name of Jesus Christ.
8. Wash me clean today O Lord by the blood of Jesus Christ.
9. I cover myself and my household with the blood of Jesus Christ.
10. My prayers today will not go in vain; my prayers will produce the desired results in the name of Jesus Christ.
11. Today I nullify every word of rejection spoken against me because I was born from unwanted pregnancy, in the name of Jesus Christ.
12. Today I nullify every word of rejection spoken against me because I was born when my parents were having financial difficulties, in the name of Jesus Christ.
13. Today I nullify every word of rejection spoken against me because I was born from an incestuous relationship, in the name of Jesus Christ.
14. Today I nullify every word of rejection spoken against me because I was born from an unplanned pregnancy, in the name of Jesus Christ.
15. Today I nullify every word of rejection spoken against me because I was a child of a drug addict, in the name of Jesus Christ.

16. Today I nullify every word of rejection spoken against me because I was a child of an alcoholic, in the name of Jesus Christ.
17. Today I nullify every word of rejection spoken against me because my parents get divorced when I was in my mother's womb, in the name of Jesus Christ
18. Today I nullify every word of rejection spoken against me because my father refused to accept me as his own child when I was born, in the name of Jesus Christ.
19. Today I nullify every word of rejection spoken against me because I was born out of an adulterous affair, in the name of Jesus Christ.
20. Today I nullify every word of rejection spoken against me when I made mistakes as a child, in the name of Jesus Christ.
21. Today I nullify every spoken word of rejection that has been following me around, in the name of Jesus Christ.
22. Evil effects of any word of rejection that are still manifesting in my life; be nullified now by the blood of Jesus Christ.
23. Evil effects of any word of rejection that are still manifesting in my family; be nullified now by the blood of Jesus Christ.
24. Evil effects of any word of rejection that are still manifesting in my marriage; be nullified now by the blood of Jesus Christ.
25. Evil effects of any word of rejection that are still manifesting in my business; be nullified now by the blood of Jesus Christ.
26. Evil effects of any word of rejection that are still manifesting in the life of my spouse; be nullified now by the blood of Jesus Christ.

27. Evil effects of any word of rejection that are still manifesting in the lives of my children; be nullified now by the blood of Jesus Christ.
28. Evil effects of any word of rejection that are still manifesting in my finances; be nullified now by the blood of Jesus Christ.
29. Every collective yoke of rejection that has caged my life, I command you to release me now by the power and authority in the name of Jesus Christ.
30. Every collective yoke of rejection that has caged my destiny, I command you to release me now by the power and authority in the name of Jesus Christ.
31. Parental rejection that has put me in continuous sorrow, I command you to break now by the power and authority in the name of Jesus Christ.
32. By the power and authority in the blood of Jesus Christ, today I recover every good thing that I have lost in life, in the name of Jesus Christ.
33. By the power and authority in the blood of Jesus Christ, today I recover every blessing that I have lost in life, in the name of Jesus Christ.
34. By the power and authority in the blood of Jesus Christ, today I recover every opportunity that I have lost in life, in the name of Jesus Christ.
35. By the power and authority in the blood of Jesus Christ, today I recover every miracle that I have lost in life, in the name of Jesus Christ.

DAY SEVEN

PRAYER TO CANCEL EVIL PRONOUNCEMENT

Passages To Read Before You Pray:
Isaiah 54:1-17, Ezekiel 21:26-27, Genesis 12:2-3, Psalms 3, 9, 10, 61, 69, 70, 140

I stand on the word of God to claim my right as a child of the Kingdom, I cover myself in the blood of Jesus Christ, I cover my household and everything concerning me in the blood of Jesus Christ. I hereby charge this atmosphere by the blood of Jesus Christ and by the fire of the Holy Ghost. I command fresh fire of God to rest upon me now as in the day of Pentecost, let fresh anointing and new oil be released upon me now as I pray. I receive power and authority over the power and the kingdom of darkness, to root out and to pull down, to destroy and to throw down, to build and to plant; whatever I decree in this prayer shall be established; whatever I bind today shall be bound in heaven and whatever I loose today shall be loosed in heaven as it is written in the word of God. Let fresh fire of God be released on my prayer altar and my prayer life now, prince of Persia cannot hinder my prayer, territorial spirit of my neighborhood cannot hinder my prayer, household wickedness cannot hinder my prayer.

I can see my prayer attracting divine intervention. This is the day that the Lord has made, I will rejoice and be glad in it. This is the

day that the Lord has chosen to set me free from any form of bondage and break any form of curses upon my life; this is the day that I will receive a total and complete deliverance in every area of my life, today shall mark the beginning of a new thing in my life.

I am a child of God, born of the Spirit, redeemed by the blood of the Lamb. It is written concerning me that power and authority is given unto me over all devils and to cure diseases, I hereby take authority over any form of curses upon my life, be it ancestral, be it generational, be it demon-inflicted or self-inflicted; I command all curses upon my life to break now by the authority in the name of Jesus Christ. The Bible says, where the word of a king is, there is power; today I speak as a king with the authority and power of the King of kings, and I command every other power to bow in the name of Jesus Christ. I render any power behind any curse upon my life useless and ineffective; I overcome any form of distraction, spiritual laziness and slumber, before the end of this prayer session my testimonies shall manifest without delay by the power in the name of Jesus Christ. Amen!

PRAYER POINTS

1. O God my Father, thank you for being my God, my Father and my friend.
2. O God my Father, thank you for the privilege to know you and the power of the resurrection of Jesus Christ.
3. O God my Father, thank you for always being there for me and with me.

4. O God my Father, thank you for the great and mighty things that you are doing in my life.
5. O God my Father, thank you for your provision and protection over me and my household.
6. O God my Father, thank you for always answering my prayers.
7. I confess my sins before you today and I ask you to forgive me on the basis of your mercy, in the name of Jesus Christ.
8. Wash me clean today O Lord by the blood of Jesus Christ.
9. I cover myself and my household with the blood of Jesus Christ.
10. My prayers today will not go in vain; my prayers will produce the desired results in the name of Jesus Christ.
11. Every negative word issued against me by my mother, be nullified by the blood of Jesus Christ.
12. Every negative word issued against me by my father, be nullified by the blood of Jesus Christ.
13. Every negative word issued against me by my stepmother, be nullified by the blood of Jesus Christ.
14. Every negative word issued against me by my stepfather, be nullified by the blood of Jesus Christ.
15. Every negative word issued against me by my grandparent, be nullified by the blood of Jesus Christ.
16. Every selective rejection working against me, release me now by the power and authority in the name of Jesus Christ.
17. By the power and authority in the blood of Jesus Christ, I decree today that wherever I have been rejected, I will be accepted in the name of Jesus Christ.

18. By the power and authority in the blood of Jesus Christ, today I decree that wherever I have been denied, I will be approved in the name of Jesus Christ.
19. By the power and authority in the blood of Jesus Christ, today I decree that wherever I have been turned down, I will be welcomed in the name of Jesus Christ.
20. By the power and authority in the blood of Jesus Christ, today I decree that whenever people are saying there is casting down, I will sing there is lifting up in the name of Jesus Christ.
21. By the power and authority in the blood of Jesus Christ, today I decree that wherever I have been disgraced, I will be celebrated in the name of Jesus Christ.
22. By the power and authority in the blood of Jesus Christ, any situation in my life causing me to be sorrowful will bring me joy and happiness, in the name of Jesus Christ.
23. By the power and authority in the blood of Jesus Christ, today I decree that instead of ridicule I will receive miracles in every area of my life, in the name of Jesus Christ.
24. Every handwriting of rejection upon my life; be completely wiped off by the blood of Jesus Christ, in the name of Jesus Christ.
25. Every handwriting of rejection upon my family; be completely wiped off by the blood of Jesus Christ, in the name of Jesus Christ.
26. Every handwriting of rejection upon my spouse; be completely wiped off by the blood of Jesus Christ, in the name of Jesus Christ.
27. Every handwriting of rejection upon my children; be completely wiped off by the blood of Jesus Christ, in the name of Jesus Christ.

28. Every handwriting of rejection upon my business; be completely wiped off by the blood of Jesus Christ, in the name of Jesus Christ.
29. Every handwriting of rejection upon my finances; be completely wiped off by the blood of Jesus Christ, in the name of Jesus Christ.
30. Every handwriting of rejection upon my destiny; be completely wiped off by the blood of Jesus Christ, in the name of Jesus Christ.
31. Every curse of rejection upon my life sponsored by the household wickedness, I command you to break now by the power and authority in the name of Jesus Christ.
32. Every curse of rejection upon my life sponsored by the power of witchcraft, I command you to break now by the power and authority in the name of Jesus Christ.
33. Every curse of rejection upon my life sponsored by Pharaoh of my father's house, I command you to break now by the power and authority in the name of Jesus Christ.
34. Every curse of rejection upon my life sponsored by principalities and powers, I command you to break now by the power and authority in the name of Jesus Christ.
35. Every curse of rejection upon my life sponsored by Jezebel spirit, I command you to break now by the power and authority in the name of Jesus Christ.
36. Every curse of rejection upon my life sponsored by unrepentant enemies, I command you to break now by the power and authority in the name of Jesus Christ.

DELIVERANCE FROM GENERATIONAL CURSES OF FAILURE

(5 DAYS FASTING & INTENSIVE PRAYER)

KEY BIBLE PASSAGE

"And Moses went up from the plains of Moab unto the mountain of Nebo, to the top of Pisgah, that is over against Jericho. And the LORD shewed him all the land of Gilead, unto Dan, And all Naphtali, and the land of Ephraim, and Manasseh, and all the land of Judah, unto the utmost sea, And the south, and the plain of the valley of Jericho, the city of palm trees, unto Zoar.

And the LORD said unto him, This is the land which I sware unto Abraham, unto Isaac, and unto Jacob, saying, I will give it unto thy seed: I have caused thee to see it with thine eyes, but thou shalt not go over thither. So Moses the servant of the LORD died there in the land of Moab, according to the word of the LORD." – Deuteronomy 34:1-5

DAY ONE

GENERATIONAL REPENTANCE

Passages To Read Before You Pray:
Exodus 20:1-5, Jeremiah 31:27-34, Daniel 9:1-19, Psalms 89

I stand on the word of God to claim my right as a child of the Kingdom, I cover myself in the blood of Jesus Christ, I cover my household and everything concerning me in the blood of Jesus Christ. I hereby charge this atmosphere by the blood of Jesus Christ and by the fire of the Holy Ghost. I command fresh fire of God to rest upon me now as in the day of Pentecost, let fresh anointing and new oil be released upon me now as I pray. I receive power and authority over the power and the kingdom of darkness, to root out and to pull down, to destroy and to throw down, to build and to plant; whatever I decree in this prayer shall be established; whatever I bind today shall be bound in heaven and whatever I loose today shall be loosed in heaven as it is written in the word of God. Let fresh fire of God be released on my prayer altar and my prayer life now, prince of Persia cannot hinder my prayer, territorial spirit of my neighborhood cannot hinder my prayer, household wickedness cannot hinder my prayer.

I can see my prayer attracting divine intervention. This is the day that the Lord has made, I will rejoice and be glad in it. This is the day that the Lord has chosen to set me free from any form of

bondage and break any form of curses upon my life; this is the day that I will receive a total and complete deliverance in every area of my life, today shall mark the beginning of a new thing in my life.

I am a child of God, born of the Spirit, redeemed by the blood of the Lamb. It is written concerning me that power and authority is given unto me over all devils and to cure diseases, I hereby take authority over any form of curses upon my life, be it ancestral, be it generational, be it demon-inflicted or self-inflicted; I command all curses upon my life to break now by the authority in the name of Jesus Christ. The Bible says, where the word of a king is, there is power; today I speak as a king with the authority and power of the King of kings, and I command every other power to bow in the name of Jesus Christ. I render any power behind any curse upon my life useless and ineffective; I overcome any form of distraction, spiritual laziness and slumber, before the end of this prayer session my testimonies shall manifest without delay by the power in the name of Jesus Christ. Amen!

PRAYER POINTS

1. God my Father, thank you for being my God, my Father and my friend.
2. God my Father, thank you for the privilege to know you and the power of the resurrection of Jesus Christ.
3. God my Father, thank you for always being there for me and with me.
4. God my Father, thank you for the great and mighty things that you are doing in my life.

5. God my Father, thank you for your provision and protection over me and my household.
6. God my Father, thank you for always answering my prayers.
7. God my Father, I confess and repent of all sins in my life or my ancestors' lives that have resulted in a curse upon my life or bloodline; forgive me Lord on the basis of your mercy and cleanse me by the blood of Jesus Christ.
8. God my Father, I confess today and repent of all sins of disobedience in my life or my ancestor's lives that have resulted in a curse upon my life or bloodline; forgive me Lord on the basis of your mercy and cleanse me by the blood of Jesus Christ.
9. God my Father, I confess today and repent of all sins of rebellion in my life or my ancestor's lives that have resulted in a curse upon my life or bloodline; forgive me Lord on the basis of your mercy and cleanse me by the blood of Jesus Christ.
10. God my Father, I confess today and repent of all sins of perversion in my life or my ancestor's lives that have resulted in a curse upon my life or bloodline; forgive me Lord on the basis of your mercy and cleanse me by the blood of Jesus Christ.
11. God my Father, I confess today and repent of all sins of witchcraft in my life or my ancestor's lives that have resulted in a curse upon my life or bloodline; forgive me Lord on the basis of your mercy and cleanse me by the blood of Jesus Christ.
12. God my Father, I confess today and repent of all sins of idolatry in my life or my ancestor's lives that have resulted in a curse upon my life or bloodline; forgive

me Lord on the basis of your mercy and cleanse me by the blood of Jesus Christ.
13. God my Father, I confess today and repent of all sins of lust in my life or my ancestor's lives that have resulted in a curse upon my life or bloodline; forgive me Lord on the basis of your mercy and cleanse me by the blood of Jesus Christ.
14. God my Father, I confess today and repent of all sins of adultery in my life or my ancestor's lives that have resulted in a curse upon my life or bloodline; forgive me Lord on the basis of your mercy and cleanse me by the blood of Jesus Christ.
15. God my Father, I confess today and repent of all sins of fornication in my life or my ancestor's lives that have resulted in a curse upon my life or bloodline; forgive me Lord on the basis of your mercy and cleanse me by the blood of Jesus Christ.
16. God my Father, I confess today and repent of all sins of mistreatment of others in my life or my ancestor's lives that have resulted in a curse upon my life or bloodline; forgive me Lord on the basis of your mercy and cleanse me by the blood of Jesus Christ.
17. God my Father, I confess today and repent of all sins of murder or abortion in my life or my ancestor's lives that have resulted in a curse upon my life or bloodline; forgive me Lord on the basis of your mercy and cleanse me by the blood of Jesus Christ.
18. God my Father, I confess today and repent of all sins of cheating in my life or my ancestor's lives that have resulted in a curse upon my life or bloodline; forgive me Lord on the basis of your mercy and cleanse me by the blood of Jesus Christ.

19. God my Father, I confess today and repent of all sins of lying in my life or my ancestor's lives that have resulted in a curse upon my life or bloodline; forgive me Lord on the basis of your mercy and cleanse me by the blood of Jesus Christ.
20. God my Father, I confess today and repent of all sins of sorcery in my life or my ancestor's lives that have resulted in a curse upon my life or bloodline; forgive me Lord on the basis of your mercy and cleanse me by the blood of Jesus Christ.
21. God my Father, I confess today and repent of all sins of divination in my life or my ancestor's lives that have resulted in a curse upon my life or bloodline; forgive me Lord on the basis of your mercy and cleanse me by the blood of Jesus Christ.
22. God my Father, I confess today and repent of all sins of occult involvement in my life or my ancestor's lives that have resulted in a curse upon my life or bloodline; forgive me Lord on the basis of your mercy and cleanse me by the blood of Jesus Christ.
23. I disassociate myself from all evil done by my ancestors by the power in the blood of Jesus Christ.
24. I disassociate myself from all evil attitudes done by my ancestors against the will and purpose of God, in the name of Jesus Christ.
25. With all my heart I disagree with all sins committed by my ancestors, Father Lord have mercy and cleanse me by the blood of Jesus Christ.
26. Today with all my heart I declare that I refuse to be like my parents, in the name of Jesus Christ.
27. Today with all my heart I declare that I refuse to be like any of my ancestors, in the name of Jesus Christ.

28. I refuse to suffer the same problems as my parents, I reject it; my heart, soul, spirit and body reject it in the name of Jesus Christ.
29. I refuse to suffer the same problems as any of my ancestors, I reject it; my heart, soul, spirit and body reject it in the name of Jesus Christ.
30. In the name of Jesus Christ, I refuse to go through what my parents went through, my case is different, I am a child of God and covered by the blood of Jesus Christ.
31. By the power and authority in the blood of Jesus Christ, I sever myself from my bloodline, in the name of Jesus Christ.
32. By the power and authority in the blood of Jesus Christ, I sever myself from the connection to any of my ancestors, in the name of Jesus Christ.
33. By the power and authority in the blood of Jesus Christ, I sever myself from spiritual connection to any of my ancestors, in the name of Jesus Christ.
34. By the power and authority in the blood of Jesus Christ, I sever myself from physical connection to any of my ancestors, in the name of Jesus Christ.
35. By the power and authority in the blood of Jesus Christ, I sever myself from emotional connection to any of my ancestors, in the name of Jesus Christ.
36. By the power and authority in the blood of Jesus Christ, I sever myself from mental connection to any of my ancestors, in the name of Jesus Christ.
37. By the power and authority in the blood of Jesus Christ, I sever myself from the connection to the idol of my father's house, in the name of Jesus Christ.

38. By the power and authority in the blood of Jesus Christ, I sever myself from the connection to the idol of my mother's house, in the name of Jesus Christ.
39. By the power and authority in the blood of Jesus Christ, I destroy every spiritual DNA that links me to my ancestors by the fire of God, in the name of Jesus Christ.
40. By the power and authority in the blood of Jesus Christ, I destroy every spiritual DNA that links my children to my ancestors by the fire of God, in the name of Jesus Christ.

DAY TWO

PRAYER TO BREAK CYCLE OF FAILURE

Passages To Read Before You Pray:
Galatians 3:13, Joshua 1:1-18, Psalms 46, 86, 29, 59. 69

I stand on the word of God to claim my right as a child of the Kingdom, I cover myself in the blood of Jesus Christ, I cover my household and everything concerning me in the blood of Jesus Christ. I hereby charge this atmosphere by the blood of Jesus Christ and by the fire of the Holy Ghost. I command fresh fire of God to rest upon me now as in the day of Pentecost, let fresh anointing and new oil be released upon me now as I pray. I receive power and authority over the power and the kingdom of darkness, to root out and to pull down, to destroy and to throw down, to build and to plant; whatever I decree in this prayer shall be established; whatever I bind today shall be bound in heaven and whatever I loose today shall be loosed in heaven as it is written in the word of God. Let fresh fire of God be released on my prayer altar and my prayer life now, prince of Persia cannot hinder my prayer, territorial spirit of my neighborhood cannot hinder my prayer, household wickedness cannot hinder my prayer.

I can see my prayer attracting divine intervention. This is the day that the Lord has made, I will rejoice and be glad in it. This is the day that the Lord has chosen to set me free from any form of

bondage and break any form of curses upon my life; this is the day that I will receive a total and complete deliverance in every area of my life, today shall mark the beginning of a new thing in my life.

I am a child of God, born of the Spirit, redeemed by the blood of the Lamb. It is written concerning me that power and authority is given unto me over all devils and to cure diseases, I hereby take authority over any form of curses upon my life, be it ancestral, be it generational, be it demon-inflicted or self-inflicted; I command all curses upon my life to break now by the authority in the name of Jesus Christ. The Bible says, where the word of a king is, there is power; today I speak as a king with the authority and power of the King of kings, and I command every other power to bow in the name of Jesus Christ. I render any power behind any curse upon my life useless and ineffective; I overcome any form of distraction, spiritual laziness and slumber, before the end of this prayer session my testimonies shall manifest without delay by the power in the name of Jesus Christ. Amen!

PRAYER POINTS

1. God my Father, thank you for being my God, my Father and my friend.
2. God my Father, thank you for the privilege to know you and the power of the resurrection of Jesus Christ.
3. God my Father, thank you for always being there for me and with me.
4. God my Father, thank you for the great and mighty things that you are doing in my life.

5. God my Father, thank you for your provision and protection over me and my household.
6. God my Father, thank you for always answering my prayers.
7. I confess my sins before you today and I ask you to forgive me on the basis of your mercy, in the name of Jesus Christ.
8. Wash me clean today O Lord by the blood of Jesus Christ.
9. I cover myself and my household with the blood of Jesus Christ.
10. My prayers today will not go in vain; my prayers will produce the desired results in the name of Jesus Christ.
11. I take authority and break every curse of failure upon my life in the name of Jesus Christ.
12. By the power in the of blood of Jesus Christ I break every curse of failure in my bloodline from my life to my past generations all the way to Adam the first man, in the name of Jesus Christ.
13. By the power in the blood of Jesus Christ I break every curse of failure over my children and their children and children's children, in the name of Jesus Christ.
14. I take authority and break the curse of failure at the edge of miracle, in the name of Jesus Christ.
15. I take authority and break every curse of failure at the point of breakthrough, in the name of Jesus Christ.
16. I take authority and break every curse of failure holding my life down, in the name of Jesus Christ.
17. I take authority and break every curse of failure causing my life to be stagnated, in the name of Jesus Christ.
18. I take authority and break every curse of failure causing my life to go backward, in the name of Jesus Christ.

19. I take authority and break every curse of failure causing me to live a miserable life, in the name of Jesus Christ.
20. I take authority and break every curse of failure causing me to lose every opportunity that comes my way, in the name of Jesus Christ.
21. I take authority and break every curse of failure causing me to lose divine helpers that God has sent to help me, in the name of Jesus Christ.
22. I take authority and break every curse of failure keeping me at the bottom of the ladder, in the name of Jesus Christ.
23. I take authority and break every cycle of failure in any area of my life, in the name of Jesus Christ.
24. I take authority and break every cycle of failure in marriage, in the name of Jesus Christ.
25. I take authority and break every cycle of failure manifesting in the life of my spouse in the name of Jesus Christ.
26. I take authority and break every cycle of failure manifesting in the life of my children, in the name of Jesus Christ.
27. I take authority and break every cycle of failure manifesting in my business, in the name of Jesus Christ.
28. I take authority and break every cycle of failure manifesting in my finances, in the name of Jesus Christ.
29. I take authority and break every cycle of failure concerning all my relationships, in the name of Jesus Christ.
30. I take authority and break every cycle of failure that will not allow me to get marry, in the name of Jesus Christ.

31. I take authority and break every cycle of failure that will not allow me to have a successful and stable relationship, in the name of Jesus Christ.
32. I take authority and break every cycle of failure that will not allow me to have a good and stable employment, in the name of Jesus Christ.
33. Every curse of last minute failure, enough is enough, I command you to break now by the power in the name of Jesus Christ.
34. Every curse of last minute failure in the life of my spouse, enough is enough, I command you to break now by the power in the name of Jesus Christ.
35. Every curse of last minute failure in the life of my children, enough is enough, I command you to break now by the power in the name of Jesus Christ.
36. Every curse of last minute failure in my finances, enough is enough, I command you to break now by the power in the name of Jesus Christ.
37. Every curse of last minute failure working against my breakthrough, enough is enough, I command you to break now by the power in the name of Jesus Christ.
38. Every curse of last minute failure working against my miracles, enough is enough, I command you to break now by the power in the name of Jesus Christ.

DAY THREE

PRAYER AGAINST LAST MINUTE FAILURE

Passages To Read Before You Pray:
Exodus 14:13-14, Psalms 19, 29, 42, 59, 69, 34

I stand on the word of God to claim my right as a child of the Kingdom, I cover myself in the blood of Jesus Christ, I cover my household and everything concerning me in the blood of Jesus Christ. I hereby charge this atmosphere by the blood of Jesus Christ and by the fire of the Holy Ghost. I command fresh fire of God to rest upon me now as in the day of Pentecost, let fresh anointing and new oil be released upon me now as I pray. I receive power and authority over the power and the kingdom of darkness, to root out and to pull down, to destroy and to throw down, to build and to plant; whatever I decree in this prayer shall be established; whatever I bind today shall be bound in heaven and whatever I loose today shall be loosed in heaven as it is written in the word of God. Let fresh fire of God be released on my prayer altar and my prayer life now, prince of Persia cannot hinder my prayer, territorial spirit of my neighborhood cannot hinder my prayer, household wickedness cannot hinder my prayer.

I can see my prayer attracting divine intervention. This is the day that the Lord has made, I will rejoice and be glad in it. This is the day that the Lord has chosen to set me free from any form of

bondage and break any form of curses upon my life; this is the day that I will receive a total and complete deliverance in every area of my life, today shall mark the beginning of a new thing in my life.

I am a child of God, born of the Spirit, redeemed by the blood of the Lamb. It is written concerning me that power and authority is given unto me over all devils and to cure diseases, I hereby take authority over any form of curses upon my life, be it ancestral, be it generational, be it demon-inflicted or self-inflicted; I command all curses upon my life to break now by the authority in the name of Jesus Christ. The Bible says, where the word of a king is, there is power; today I speak as a king with the authority and power of the King of kings, and I command every other power to bow in the name of Jesus Christ. I render any power behind any curse upon my life useless and ineffective; I overcome any form of distraction, spiritual laziness and slumber, before the end of this prayer session my testimonies shall manifest without delay by the power in the name of Jesus Christ. Amen!

PRAYER POINTS

1. O God my Father, thank you for being my God, my Father and my friend.
2. O God my Father, thank you for the privilege to know you and the power of the resurrection of Jesus Christ.
3. O God my Father, thank you for always being there for me and with me.
4. O God my Father, thank you for the great and mighty things that you are doing in my life.

5. O God my Father, thank you for your provision and protection over me and my household.
6. O God my Father, thank you for always answering my prayers.
7. I confess my sins before you today and I ask you to forgive me on the basis of your mercy, in the name of Jesus Christ.
8. Wash me clean today O Lord by the blood of Jesus Christ.
9. I cover myself and my household with the blood of Jesus Christ.
10. My prayers today will not go in vain; my prayers will produce the desired results in the name of Jesus Christ.
11. Every curse of last minute failure working against God's plans in my life, enough is enough, I command you to break now by the power in the name of Jesus Christ.
12. Every curse of last minute failure working against my dreams, enough is enough, I command you to break now by the power in the name of Jesus Christ.
13. Every curse of last minute failure working against my academic success, enough is enough, I command you to break now by the power in the name of Jesus Christ.
14. Every curse of last minute failure working against my business success, enough is enough, I command you to break now by the power in the name of Jesus Christ.
15. Every curse of last minute failure working against my ministerial success, enough is enough, I command you to break now by the power in the name of Jesus Christ.
16. Every curse of last minute failure working against my financial breakthroughs, enough is enough, I command you to break now by the power in the name of Jesus Christ.

17. Every curse of last minute failure blocking me from having financial freedom, enough is enough, I command you to break now by the power in the name of Jesus Christ.
18. The spirit of last minute failure upon my life, I utterly destroy you by the fire of God in the name of Jesus Christ.
19. The spirit of last minute failure affecting my children, I utterly destroy you by the fire of God, in the name of Jesus Christ.
20. The spirit of last minute failure affecting my spouse, I utterly destroy you by the fire of God, in the name of Jesus Christ.
21. The spirit of last minute failure affecting my family, I utterly destroy you by the fire of God, in the name of Jesus Christ.
22. The spirit of last minute failure affecting my destiny, I utterly destroy you by the fire of God, in the name of Jesus Christ.
23. The spirit of last minute failure affecting my business, I utterly destroy you by the fire of God, in the name of Jesus Christ.
24. The spirit of last minute failure affecting my marriage, I utterly destroy you by the fire of God, in the name of Jesus Christ.
25. The spirit of last minute failure affecting my finances, I utterly destroy you by the fire of God in the name of Jesus Christ.
26. The spirit of last minute failure affecting my dreams, I utterly destroy you by the fire of God, in the name of Jesus Christ.

27. The spirit of last minute failure affecting God's promises in my life, I utterly destroy you by the fire of God, in the name of Jesus Christ.
28. The spirit of last minute failure in my bloodline, I command you to loose your hold upon my life, my case is different, in the name of Jesus Christ.
29. The spirit of last minute failure in my bloodline, I command you to loose your hold upon me, I am a child of God, in the name of Jesus Christ.
30. Almost there but never there is a curse, I stand on the Word of God and break this curse that is manifesting in my life by the power in the name of Jesus Christ.
31. Almost there but never there is a curse, I stand on the Word of God and break this curse that is manifesting in my family by the power in the name of Jesus Christ.
32. Almost there but never there is a curse, I stand on the Word of God and break this curse that is manifesting in my marriage by the power in the name of Jesus Christ.
33. Almost there but never there is a curse, I stand on the Word of God and break this curse that is manifesting in the life of my spouse by the power in the name of Jesus Christ.
34. Almost there but never there is a curse, I stand on the Word of God and break this curse that is manifesting in the life of my children by the power in the name of Jesus Christ.
35. Almost there but never there is a curse, I stand on the Word of God and break this curse that is manifesting in the life of my parents by the power in the name of Jesus Christ.
36. Almost there but never there is a curse, I stand on the Word of God and break this curse that is manifesting in

the life of my grandchildren by the power in the name of Jesus Christ.
37. Almost there but never there is a curse, I stand on the Word of God and break this curse that is manifesting in the life of everyone around me by the power in the name of Jesus Christ.
38. Almost there but never there is a curse, I stand on the Word of God and break this curse that is manifesting in my finances by the power in the name of Jesus Christ.
39. Almost there but never there is a curse, I stand on the Word of God and break this curse that is manifesting in my business by the power in the name of Jesus Christ.

DAY FOUR

DELIVERANCE FROM THE SPIRIT OF ALMOST THERE

Passages To Read Before You Pray:
Obadiah 1:17, Isaiah 10:27, Galatians 3:13, Psalms 35, 55, 10, 57, 83

I stand on the word of God to claim my right as a child of the Kingdom, I cover myself in the blood of Jesus Christ, I cover my household and everything concerning me in the blood of Jesus Christ. I hereby charge this atmosphere by the blood of Jesus Christ and by the fire of the Holy Ghost. I command fresh fire of God to rest upon me now as in the day of Pentecost, let fresh anointing and new oil be released upon me now as I pray. I receive power and authority over the power and the kingdom of darkness, to root out and to pull down, to destroy and to throw down, to build and to plant; whatever I decree in this prayer shall be established; whatever I bind today shall be bound in heaven and whatever I loose today shall be loosed in heaven as it is written in the word of God. Let fresh fire of God be released on my prayer altar and my prayer life now, prince of Persia cannot hinder my prayer, territorial spirit of my neighborhood cannot hinder my prayer, household wickedness cannot hinder my prayer.

I can see my prayer attracting divine intervention. This is the day that the Lord has made, I will rejoice and be glad in it. This is the

day that the Lord has chosen to set me free from any form of bondage and break any form of curses upon my life; this is the day that I will receive a total and complete deliverance in every area of my life, today shall mark the beginning of a new thing in my life.

I am a child of God, born of the Spirit, redeemed by the blood of the Lamb. It is written concerning me that power and authority is given unto me over all devils and to cure diseases, I hereby take authority over any form of curses upon my life, be it ancestral, be it generational, be it demon-inflicted or self-inflicted; I command all curses upon my life to break now by the authority in the name of Jesus Christ. The Bible says, where the word of a king is, there is power; today I speak as a king with the authority and power of the King of kings, and I command every other power to bow in the name of Jesus Christ. I render any power behind any curse upon my life useless and ineffective; I overcome any form of distraction, spiritual laziness and slumber, before the end of this prayer session my testimonies shall manifest without delay by the power in the name of Jesus Christ. Amen!

PRAYER POINTS

1. O God my Father, thank you for being my God, my Father and my friend.
2. O God my Father, thank you for the privilege to know you and the power of the resurrection of Jesus Christ.
3. O God my Father, thank you for always being there for me and with me.

4. O God my Father, thank you for the great and mighty things that you are doing in my life.
5. O God my Father, thank you for your provision and protection over me and my household.
6. O God my Father, thank you for always answering my prayers.
7. I confess my sins before you today and I ask you to forgive me on the basis of your mercy, in the name of Jesus Christ.
8. Wash me clean today O Lord by the blood of Jesus Christ.
9. I cover myself and my household with the blood of Jesus Christ.
10. My prayers today will not go in vain; my prayers will produce the desired results in the name of Jesus Christ.
11. Seeing it but not receiving it is not for me, I therefore see and receive the blessings of the Lord over my life by the power in the name of Jesus Christ.
12. Seeing it but not receiving it is not for me, I therefore see and receive the blessings of the Lord over my family by the power in the name of Jesus Christ.
13. Seeing it but not receiving it is not for me, I therefore see and receive the blessings of the Lord over my marriage by the power in the name of Jesus Christ.
14. Seeing it but not receiving it is not for me, I therefore see and receive the blessings of the Lord concerning my business by the power in the name of Jesus Christ.
15. Seeing it but not receiving it is not for me, I therefore see and receive the blessings of the Lord concerning my finances by the power in the name of Jesus Christ.

16. Seeing it but not receiving it is not for me, I therefore see and receive the blessings of the Lord concerning my future by the power in the name of Jesus Christ.
17. Seeing it but not receiving it is not for me, I therefore see and receive the blessings of the Lord concerning my destiny by the power in the name of Jesus Christ.
18. Seeing it but not receiving it is not for me, I therefore see and receive the blessings of the Lord concerning my goals and dreams by the power in the name of Jesus Christ.
19. Seeing it but not receiving it is not for me, I therefore see and receive the blessings of the Lord concerning my spouse by the power in the name of Jesus Christ.
20. Seeing it but not receiving it is not for me, I therefore see and receive the blessings of the Lord concerning my children by the power in the name of Jesus Christ.
21. I cut off any connection which my life may have with the spirit of last minute failure, in the name of Jesus Christ.
22. I cut off any connection which my life may have with the spirit of last minute failure from my father's lineage by the fire of God, in the name of Jesus Christ.
23. I cut off any connection which my life may have with the spirit of last minute failure from my mother's lineage by the fire of God, in the name of Jesus Christ.
24. I destroy every agent of failure assigned to work against me by the fire of God, in the name of Jesus Christ
25. I destroy every agent of failure that has been working in my bloodline from generation to generation by the fire of God, in the name of Jesus Christ.

26. I destroy every agent of failure assigned to work against my spouse by the fire of God, in the name of Jesus Christ.
27. I destroy every agent of failure assigned to work against my children by the fire of God, in the name of Jesus Christ.
28. I destroy every agent of failure assigned to work against my future generations by the fire of God, in the name of Jesus Christ.
29. O God my Father, let the satanic mandate calculated to bring chaos at the edge of my breakthrough be nullified by the power in the name of Jesus Christ.
30. O God my Father, let the satanic mandate calculated to bring chaos at the edge of my success be nullified by the power in the name of Jesus Christ.
31. O God my Father, let the satanic mandate calculated to bring chaos at the edge of my miracle be nullified by the power in the name of Jesus Christ.
32. O God my Father, let the satanic mandate calculated to bring chaos at the edge of my testimony be nullified by the power in the name of Jesus Christ.
33. O God my Father, arise and destroy every challenge at the edge of my testimony, in the name of Jesus Christ.
34. O God my Father, arise and destroy every challenge at the edge of my miracle, in the name of Jesus Christ.
35. O God my Father, arise and destroy every challenge at the edge of my breakthrough, in the name of Jesus Christ.
36. O God my Father, arise and destroy every challenge at the point of my promotion, in the name of Jesus Christ.
37. O God my Father, arise and destroy every challenge at the edge of my success, in the name of Jesus Christ.

38. O God my Father, arise and destroy every challenge at the edge of my financial freedom, in the name of Jesus Christ.
39. O God my Father, arise and destroy every challenge at the edge of my business success, in the name of Jesus Christ.
40. O God my Father, arise and destroy every challenge at the edge of my ministerial success, in the name of Jesus Christ.

DAY FIVE

DELIVERANCE FROM ANCESTRAL CURSE OF FAILURE

Passages To Read Before You Pray:
Jeremiah 31:27-32, Joel 2:21-27, Psalms 55, 109, 128, 70, 103, 106

I stand on the word of God to claim my right as a child of the Kingdom, I cover myself in the blood of Jesus Christ, I cover my household and everything concerning me in the blood of Jesus Christ. I hereby charge this atmosphere by the blood of Jesus Christ and by the fire of the Holy Ghost. I command fresh fire of God to rest upon me now as in the day of Pentecost, let fresh anointing and new oil be released upon me now as I pray. I receive power and authority over the power and the kingdom of darkness, to root out and to pull down, to destroy and to throw down, to build and to plant; whatever I decree in this prayer shall be established; whatever I bind today shall be bound in heaven and whatever I loose today shall be loosed in heaven as it is written in the word of God. Let fresh fire of God be released on my prayer altar and my prayer life now, prince of Persia cannot hinder my prayer, territorial spirit of my neighborhood cannot hinder my prayer, household wickedness cannot hinder my prayer.

I can see my prayer attracting divine intervention. This is the day that the Lord has made, I will rejoice and be glad in it. This is the day that the Lord has chosen to set me free from any form of bondage and break any form of curses upon my life; this is the day that I will receive a total and complete deliverance in every area of my life, today shall mark the beginning of a new thing in my life.

I am a child of God, born of the Spirit, redeemed by the blood of the Lamb. It is written concerning me that power and authority is given unto me over all devils and to cure diseases, I hereby take authority over any form of curses upon my life, be it ancestral, be it generational, be it demon-inflicted or self-inflicted; I command all curses upon my life to break now by the authority in the name of Jesus Christ. The Bible says, where the word of a king is, there is power; today I speak as a king with the authority and power of the King of kings, and I command every other power to bow in the name of Jesus Christ. I render any power behind any curse upon my life useless and ineffective; I overcome any form of distraction, spiritual laziness and slumber, before the end of this prayer session my testimonies shall manifest without delay by the power in the name of Jesus Christ. Amen!

PRAYER POINTS

1. O God my Father, thank you for being my God, my Father and my friend.
2. O God my Father, thank you for the privilege to know you and the power of the resurrection of Jesus Christ.

3. O God my Father, thank you for always being there for me and with me.
4. O God my Father, thank you for the great and mighty things that you are doing in my life.
5. O God my Father, thank you for your provision and protection over me and my household.
6. O God my Father, thank you for always answering my prayers.
7. I confess my sins before you today and I ask you to forgive me on the basis of your mercy, in the name of Jesus Christ.
8. Wash me clean today O Lord by the blood of Jesus Christ.
9. I cover myself and my household with the blood of Jesus Christ.
10. My prayers today will not go in vain; my prayers will produce the desired results in the name of Jesus Christ.
11. O God my Father, arise and scatter every evil gathering at the edge of my breakthrough by your fire, in the name of Jesus Christ.
12. O God my Father, arise and scatter every evil gathering at the edge of my miracle by your fire, in the name of Jesus Christ.
13. O God my Father, arise and scatter every evil gathering at the edge of my testimony by your fire, in the name of Jesus Christ.
14. O God my Father, arise and scatter every evil gathering at the edge of my success by your fire, in the name of Jesus Christ.
15. O God my Father, arise and scatter every evil gathering at the edge of my ministerial success by your fire, in the name of Jesus Christ.

16. O God my Father, arise and scatter every evil gathering at the edge of my promotion by your fire, in the name of Jesus Christ.
17. O God my Father, arise and scatter every evil gathering at the edge of my business success by your fire, in the name of Jesus Christ.
18. O God my Father, arise and scatter every evil gathering at the edge of my financial freedom by your fire, in the name of Jesus Christ.
19. O God my Father, arise and scatter every evil gathering at the point of my open heavens by your fire, in the name of Jesus Christ.
20. The curse of failure is broken, the hour of my breakthrough is now, my breakthrough stand sure for the Lord of hosts has spoken good concerning me, it is well with me in the name of Jesus Christ.
21. The curse of failure is broken, the hour of my miracle is now, my miracle stand sure for the Lord of hosts has spoken good concerning me, it is well with me in the name of Jesus Christ.
22. The curse of failure is broken, the hour of my promotion is now, my promotion stand sure for the Lord of hosts has spoken good concerning me, it is well with me in the name of Jesus Christ.
23. The curse of failure is broken, the hour of my success is now, my success stand sure for the Lord of hosts has spoken good concerning me, it is well with me in the name of Jesus Christ.
24. The curse of failure is broken, the hour of my financial freedom is now, my financial freedom stand sure for the Lord of hosts has spoken good concerning me, it is well with me in the name of Jesus Christ.

25. The curse of failure is broken, the hour of my deliverance is now, my deliverance stand sure for the Lord of hosts has spoken good concerning me, it is well with me in the name of Jesus Christ.
26. The curse of failure is broken, the hour of my revelation is now, my revelation to the world stand sure for the Lord of hosts has spoken good concerning me, it is well with me in the name of Jesus Christ.
27. O God my Father, advertise your power of breakthrough in my life, let the world hear my testimony and let those who hate me rejoice with me, in the name of Jesus Christ.
28. O God my Father, advertise your power of miracle in my life, let the world hear my testimony and let those who hate me rejoice with me, in the name of Jesus Christ.
29. O God my Father, advertise your healing power in my life, let the world hear my testimony and let those who hate me rejoice with me, in the name of Jesus Christ.
30. O God my Father, advertise your power of deliverance in my life, let the world hear my testimony and let those who hate me rejoice with me, in the name of Jesus Christ.
31. O God my Father, advertise your power of uncommon favor in my life, let the world hear my testimony and let those who hate me rejoice with me, in the name of Jesus Christ.
32. O God my Father, advertise your power of supernatural increase in my life, let the world hear my testimony and let those who hate me rejoice with me, in the name of Jesus Christ.
33. I decree today that every good dream I have will come to pass in the name of Jesus Christ.

34. I decree today that every good vision I have will be fulfilled in the name of Jesus Christ.
35. I decree today that every good idea I have will come to realization in the name of Jesus Christ.
36. I decree today that every project I started must be completed in the name of Jesus Christ
37. I decree today that everything I lay my hands on shall prosper in the name of Jesus Christ.
38. The grace to rise and shine above every unfavorable situation fall on me now, in the name of Jesus Christ.

DELIVERANCE FROM ANCESTRAL CURSES OF UNTIMELY DEATH

(5 DAYS FASTING & INTENSIVE PRAYER)

KEY BIBLE PASSAGE

"I will ransom them from the power of the grave; I will redeem them from death: O death, I will be thy plagues; O grave, I will be thy destruction: repentance shall be hid from mine eyes."
– Hosea 13:14

DAY ONE

GENERATIONAL REPENTANCE

Passages To Read Before You Pray:
Exodus 20:1-5, Jeremiah 31:27-34, Daniel 9:1-19, Psalms 89

I stand on the word of God to claim my right as a child of the Kingdom, I cover myself in the blood of Jesus Christ, I cover my household and everything concerning me in the blood of Jesus Christ. I hereby charge this atmosphere by the blood of Jesus Christ and by the fire of the Holy Ghost. I command fresh fire of God to rest upon me now as in the day of Pentecost, let fresh anointing and new oil be released upon me now as I pray. I receive power and authority over the power and the kingdom of darkness, to root out and to pull down, to destroy and to throw down, to build and to plant; whatever I decree in this prayer shall be established; whatever I bind today shall be bound in heaven and whatever I loose today shall be loosed in heaven as it is written in the word of God. Let fresh fire of God be released on my prayer altar and my prayer life now, prince of Persia cannot hinder my prayer, territorial spirit of my neighborhood cannot hinder my prayer, household wickedness cannot hinder my prayer.

I can see my prayer attracting divine intervention. This is the day that the Lord has made, I will rejoice and be glad in it. This is the day that the Lord has chosen to set me free from any form of

bondage and break any form of curses upon my life; this is the day that I will receive a total and complete deliverance in every area of my life, today shall mark the beginning of a new thing in my life.

I am a child of God, born of the Spirit, redeemed by the blood of the Lamb. It is written concerning me that power and authority is given unto me over all devils and to cure diseases, I hereby take authority over any form of curses upon my life, be it ancestral, be it generational, be it demon-inflicted or self-inflicted; I command all curses upon my life to break now by the authority in the name of Jesus Christ. The Bible says, where the word of a king is, there is power; today I speak as a king with the authority and power of the King of kings, and I command every other power to bow in the name of Jesus Christ. I render any power behind any curse upon my life useless and ineffective; I overcome any form of distraction, spiritual laziness and slumber, before the end of this prayer session my testimonies shall manifest without delay by the power in the name of Jesus Christ. Amen!

PRAYER POINTS

1. God my Father, thank you for being my God, my Father and my friend.
2. God my Father, thank you for the privilege to know you and the power of the resurrection of Jesus Christ.
3. God my Father, thank you for always being there for me and with me.
4. God my Father, thank you for the great and mighty things that you are doing in my life.

5. God my Father, thank you for your provision and protection over me and my household.
6. God my Father, thank you for always answering my prayers.
7. God my Father, I confess and repent of all sins in my life or my ancestors' lives that have resulted in a curse upon my life or bloodline; forgive me Lord on the basis of your mercy and cleanse me by the blood of Jesus Christ.
8. God my Father, I confess today and repent of all sins of disobedience in my life or my ancestor's lives that have resulted in a curse upon my life or bloodline; forgive me Lord on the basis of your mercy and cleanse me by the blood of Jesus Christ.
9. God my Father, I confess today and repent of all sins of rebellion in my life or my ancestor's lives that have resulted in a curse upon my life or bloodline; forgive me Lord on the basis of your mercy and cleanse me by the blood of Jesus Christ.
10. God my Father, I confess today and repent of all sins of perversion in my life or my ancestor's lives that have resulted in a curse upon my life or bloodline; forgive me Lord on the basis of your mercy and cleanse me by the blood of Jesus Christ.
11. God my Father, I confess today and repent of all sins of witchcraft in my life or my ancestor's lives that have resulted in a curse upon my life or bloodline; forgive me Lord on the basis of your mercy and cleanse me by the blood of Jesus Christ.
12. God my Father, I confess today and repent of all sins of idolatry in my life or my ancestor's lives that have resulted in a curse upon my life or bloodline; forgive

me Lord on the basis of your mercy and cleanse me by the blood of Jesus Christ.

13. God my Father, I confess today and repent of all sins of lust in my life or my ancestor's lives that have resulted in a curse upon my life or bloodline; forgive me Lord on the basis of your mercy and cleanse me by the blood of Jesus Christ.

14. God my Father, I confess today and repent of all sins of adultery in my life or my ancestor's lives that have resulted in a curse upon my life or bloodline; forgive me Lord on the basis of your mercy and cleanse me by the blood of Jesus Christ.

15. God my Father, I confess today and repent of all sins of fornication in my life or my ancestor's lives that have resulted in a curse upon my life or bloodline; forgive me Lord on the basis of your mercy and cleanse me by the blood of Jesus Christ.

16. God my Father, I confess today and repent of all sins of mistreatment of others in my life or my ancestor's lives that have resulted in a curse upon my life or bloodline; forgive me Lord on the basis of your mercy and cleanse me by the blood of Jesus Christ.

17. God my Father, I confess today and repent of all sins of murder or abortion in my life or my ancestor's lives that have resulted in a curse upon my life or bloodline; forgive me Lord on the basis of your mercy and cleanse me by the blood of Jesus Christ.

18. God my Father, I confess today and repent of all sins of cheating in my life or my ancestor's lives that have resulted in a curse upon my life or bloodline; forgive me Lord on the basis of your mercy and cleanse me by the blood of Jesus Christ.

19. God my Father, I confess today and repent of all sins of lying in my life or my ancestor's lives that have resulted in a curse upon my life or bloodline; forgive me Lord on the basis of your mercy and cleanse me by the blood of Jesus Christ.
20. God my Father, I confess today and repent of all sins of sorcery in my life or my ancestor's lives that have resulted in a curse upon my life or bloodline; forgive me Lord on the basis of your mercy and cleanse me by the blood of Jesus Christ.
21. God my Father, I confess today and repent of all sins of divination in my life or my ancestor's lives that have resulted in a curse upon my life or bloodline; forgive me Lord on the basis of your mercy and cleanse me by the blood of Jesus Christ.
22. God my Father, I confess today and repent of all sins of occult involvement in my life or my ancestor's lives that have resulted in a curse upon my life or bloodline; forgive me Lord on the basis of your mercy and cleanse me by the blood of Jesus Christ.
23. I disassociate myself from all evil done by my ancestors by the power in the blood of Jesus Christ.
24. I disassociate myself from all evil attitudes done by my ancestors against the will and purpose of God, in the name of Jesus Christ.
25. With all my heart I disagree with all sins committed by my ancestors, Father Lord have mercy and cleanse me by the blood of Jesus Christ.
26. Today with all my heart I declare that I refuse to be like my parents, in the name of Jesus Christ.
27. Today with all my heart I declare that I refuse to be like any of my ancestors, in the name of Jesus Christ.

28. I refuse to suffer the same problems as my parents, I reject it; my heart, soul, spirit and body reject it in the name of Jesus Christ.
29. I refuse to suffer the same problems as any of my ancestors, I reject it; my heart, soul, spirit and body reject it in the name of Jesus Christ.
30. In the name of Jesus Christ, I refuse to go through what my parents went through, my case is different, I am a child of God and covered by the blood of Jesus Christ.
31. By the power and authority in the blood of Jesus Christ, I severe myself from my bloodline, in the name of Jesus Christ.
32. By the power and authority in the blood of Jesus Christ, I severe myself from the connection to any of my ancestors, in the name of Jesus Christ.
33. By the power and authority in the blood of Jesus Christ, I severe myself from spiritual connection to any of my ancestors, in the name of Jesus Christ.
34. By the power and authority in the blood of Jesus Christ, I severe myself from physical connection to any of my ancestors, in the name of Jesus Christ.
35. By the power and authority in the blood of Jesus Christ, I severe myself from emotional connection to any of my ancestors, in the name of Jesus Christ.
36. By the power and authority in the blood of Jesus Christ, I severe myself from mental connection to any of my ancestors, in the name of Jesus Christ.
37. By the power and authority in the blood of Jesus Christ, I severe myself from the connection to the idol of my father's house, in the name of Jesus Christ.

38. By the power and authority in the blood of Jesus Christ, I sever myself from the connection to the idol of my mother's house, in the name of Jesus Christ.
39. By the power and authority in the blood of Jesus Christ, I destroy every spiritual DNA that links me to my ancestors by the fire of God, in the name of Jesus Christ.
40. By the power and authority in the blood of Jesus Christ, I destroy every spiritual DNA that links my children to my ancestors by the fire of God, in the name of Jesus Christ.

DAY TWO

DELIVERANCE FROM CURSES OF UNTIMELY DEATH

Passages To Read Before You Pray:
1 Samuel 2:6, Psalms 30, 35, 61, 88, Galatians 3:13, Isaiah 10:27

I stand on the word of God to claim my right as a child of the Kingdom, I cover myself in the blood of Jesus Christ, I cover my household and everything concerning me in the blood of Jesus Christ. I hereby charge this atmosphere by the blood of Jesus Christ and by the fire of the Holy Ghost. I command fresh fire of God to rest upon me now as in the day of Pentecost, let fresh anointing and new oil be released upon me now as I pray. I receive power and authority over the power and the kingdom of darkness, to root out and to pull down, to destroy and to throw down, to build and to plant; whatever I decree in this prayer shall be established; whatever I bind today shall be bound in heaven and whatever I loose today shall be loosed in heaven as it is written in the word of God. Let fresh fire of God be released on my prayer altar and my prayer life now, prince of Persia cannot hinder my prayer, territorial spirit of my neighborhood cannot hinder my prayer, household wickedness cannot hinder my prayer.

I can see my prayer attracting divine intervention. This is the day that the Lord has made, I will rejoice and be glad in it. This is the day that the Lord has chosen to set me free from any form of

bondage and break any form of curses upon my life; this is the day that I will receive a total and complete deliverance in every area of my life, today shall mark the beginning of a new thing in my life.

I am a child of God, born of the Spirit, redeemed by the blood of the Lamb. It is written concerning me that power and authority is given unto me over all devils and to cure diseases, I hereby take authority over any form of curses upon my life, be it ancestral, be it generational, be it demon-inflicted or self-inflicted; I command all curses upon my life to break now by the authority in the name of Jesus Christ. The Bible says, where the word of a king is, there is power; today I speak as a king with the authority and power of the King of kings, and I command every other power to bow in the name of Jesus Christ. I render any power behind any curse upon my life useless and ineffective; I overcome any form of distraction, spiritual laziness and slumber, before the end of this prayer session my testimonies shall manifest without delay by the power in the name of Jesus Christ. Amen!

PRAYER POINTS

1. God my Father, thank you for being my God, my Father and my friend.
2. God my Father, thank you for the privilege to know you and the power of the resurrection of Jesus Christ.
3. God my Father, thank you for always being there for me and with me.
4. God my Father, thank you for the great and mighty things that you are doing in my life.

5. God my Father, thank you for your provision and protection over me and my household.
6. God my Father, thank you for always answering my prayers.
7. I confess my sins before you today and I ask you to forgive me on the basis of your mercy, in the name of Jesus Christ.
8. Wash me clean today O Lord by the blood of Jesus Christ.
9. I cover myself and my household with the blood of Jesus Christ.
10. My prayers today will not go in vain; my prayers will produce the desired results in the name of Jesus Christ.
11. By the power in the blood of Jesus Christ, I break every curse of untimely death in my bloodline from my life to my past generations all the way to Adam the first man, in the name of Jesus Christ.
12. I take authority and break every curse of untimely death upon my life by the power in the name of Jesus Christ.
13. I take authority and break every curse of untimely death upon my spouse by the power in the name of Jesus Christ.
14. I take authority and break every curse of untimely death upon my children by the power in the name of Jesus Christ.
15. I take authority and break every curse of untimely death upon my children's children by the power in the name of Jesus Christ.
16. I take authority and break every curse of untimely death upon my future generations by the power in the name of Jesus Christ.

17. I cut off any connection which my life may have with the spirit of untimely death by the fire of God, in the name of Jesus Christ.
18. I cut off any connection which my life may have with the spirit of untimely death from father's lineage by the fire of God, in the name of Jesus Christ.
19. I cut off any connection which my life may have with the spirit of untimely death from mother's lineage by the fire of God, in the name of Jesus Christ.
20. By the power and authority in the blood of Jesus Christ, concerning my life I cancel every appointment with untimely death, in the name of Jesus Christ.
21. By the power and authority in the blood of Jesus Christ, concerning my family I cancel every appointment with untimely death, in the name of Jesus Christ.
22. By the power and authority in the blood of Jesus Christ, concerning my marriage I cancel every appointment with untimely death, in the name of Jesus Christ.
23. By the power and authority in the blood of Jesus Christ, concerning my spouse I cancel every appointment with untimely death, in the name of Jesus Christ.
24. By the power and authority in the blood of Jesus Christ, concerning my children I cancel every appointment with untimely death, in the name of Jesus Christ.
25. By the power and authority in the blood of Jesus Christ, concerning my parents I cancel every appointment with untimely death, in the name of Jesus Christ.
26. By the power and authority in the blood of Jesus Christ, concerning my siblings I cancel every appointment with untimely death, in the name of Jesus Christ.

27. By the power and authority in the blood of Jesus Christ, concerning my friends I cancel every appointment with untimely death, in the name of Jesus Christ.
28. By the power and authority in the blood of Jesus Christ, concerning all my loved ones I cancel every appointment with untimely death, in the name of Jesus Christ.
29. Every curse of untimely death causing my ancestors to live in sorrow, you have no power over me, my case is difference, in the name of Jesus Christ.
30. Every curse of untimely death causing my ancestors to live in sorrow, you have no power over my family, loose hold upon my family now, in the name of Jesus Christ.
31. Every curse of untimely death causing my ancestors to live in sorrow, you have no power over my spouse, I command you to break now by the power in the name of Jesus Christ.
32. Every curse of untimely death causing my ancestors to live in sorrow, you have no power over my children, I command you to break now by the power in the name of Jesus Christ.
33. Every curse of untimely death causing my ancestors to live in sorrow, you have no power over my future generations, I command you to break now by the power in the name of Jesus Christ.
34. Every curse of untimely death that has been working in my bloodline from generation to generation, your time is up, I command you to break now by the power in the name of Jesus Christ.
35. Every curse of untimely death that has been taking lives of young men from the hands of their parents from

generation to generation, you have no power over my life, I command you to break now by the power in the name of Jesus Christ.
36. Every curse of untimely death that has been taking lives of young men from the hands of their parents from generation to generation, you have no power over my sons, I command you to break now by the power in the name of Jesus Christ.
37. Every curse of untimely death that has been taking lives of young men from the hands of their parents from generation to generation, you have no power over my brothers, I command you to break now by the power in the name of Jesus Christ.
38. Every curse of untimely death that has been taking lives of young men from the hands of their parents from generation to generation, you have no power over any of my loved ones, I command you to break now by the power in the name of Jesus Christ.
39. Every curse of untimely death that has been taking lives of young women from the hands of their parents from generation to generation, you have no power over my life, I command you to break now by the power in the name of Jesus Christ.
40. Every curse of untimely death that has been taking lives of young women from the hands of their parents from generation to generation, you have no power of my daughters, I command you to break now by the power in the name of Jesus Christ.
41. Every curse of untimely death that has been taking lives of young women from the hands of their parents from generation to generation, you have no power over my

sisters, I command you to break now by the power in the name of Jesus Christ.

42. Every curse of untimely death that has been taking lives of young women from the hands of their parents from generation to generation, you have no power over any of my loved ones, I command you to break now by the power in the name of Jesus Christ.

DAY THREE

DELIVERANCE FROM POWER OF THE GRAVE

Passages To Read Before You Pray:
Hosea 13:14, Isaiah 10:27, Psalms 3, 118, 9, 66, 70, 86, 69

I stand on the word of God to claim my right as a child of the Kingdom, I cover myself in the blood of Jesus Christ, I cover my household and everything concerning me in the blood of Jesus Christ. I hereby charge this atmosphere by the blood of Jesus Christ and by the fire of the Holy Ghost. I command fresh fire of God to rest upon me now as in the day of Pentecost, let fresh anointing and new oil be released upon me now as I pray. I receive power and authority over the power and the kingdom of darkness, to root out and to pull down, to destroy and to throw down, to build and to plant; whatever I decree in this prayer shall be established; whatever I bind today shall be bound in heaven and whatever I loose today shall be loosed in heaven as it is written in the word of God. Let fresh fire of God be released on my prayer altar and my prayer life now, prince of Persia cannot hinder my prayer, territorial spirit of my neighborhood cannot hinder my prayer, household wickedness cannot hinder my prayer.

I can see my prayer attracting divine intervention. This is the day that the Lord has made, I will rejoice and be glad in it. This is the day that the Lord has chosen to set me free from any form of bondage and break any form of curses upon my life; this is the day that I will receive a total and complete deliverance in every area of my life, today shall mark the beginning of a new thing in my life.

I am a child of God, born of the Spirit, redeemed by the blood of the Lamb. It is written concerning me that power and authority is given unto me over all devils and to cure diseases, I hereby take authority over any form of curses upon my life, be it ancestral, be it generational, be it demon-inflicted or self-inflicted; I command all curses upon my life to break now by the authority in the name of Jesus Christ. The Bible says, where the word of a king is, there is power; today I speak as a king with the authority and power of the King of kings, and I command every other power to bow in the name of Jesus Christ. I render any power behind any curse upon my life useless and ineffective; I overcome any form of distraction, spiritual laziness and slumber, before the end of this prayer session my testimonies shall manifest without delay by the power in the name of Jesus Christ. Amen!

PRAYER POINTS

1. O God my Father, thank you for being my God, my Father and my friend.
2. O God my Father, thank you for the privilege to know you and the power of the resurrection of Jesus Christ.
3. O God my Father, thank you for always being there for me and with me.
4. O God my Father, thank you for the great and mighty things that you are doing in my life.

5. O God my Father, thank you for your provision and protection over me and my household.
6. O God my Father, thank you for always answering my prayers.
7. I confess my sins before you today and I ask you to forgive me on the basis of your mercy, in the name of Jesus Christ.
8. Wash me clean today O Lord by the blood of Jesus Christ.
9. I cover myself and my household with the blood of Jesus Christ.
10. My prayers today will not go in vain; my prayers will produce the desired results in the name of Jesus Christ.
11. Every curse of untimely death that has been taking lives of wives from the hands of their husbands from generation to generation, you have no power over me, I command you to break now by the power in the name of Jesus Christ.
12. Every curse of untimely death that has been taking lives of wives from the hands of their husbands from generation to generation, you have no power over my daughters, I command you to break now by the power in the name of Jesus Christ.
13. Every curse of untimely death that has been taking lives of wives from the hands of their husbands from generation to generation, you have no power over my sisters, I command you to break now by the power in the name of Jesus Christ.
14. Every curse of untimely death that has been taking lives of wives from the hands of their husbands from generation to generation, you have no power over any of

my loved ones, I command you to break now by the power in the name of Jesus Christ.

15. Every curse of untimely death that has been taking lives of wives from the hands of their husbands from generation to generation, you have no power over my mother, I command you to break now by the power in the name of Jesus Christ.

16. Every curse of untimely death that has been taking lives of wives from the hands of their husbands from generation to generation, you have no power over my aunts, I command you to break now by the power in the name of Jesus Christ.

17. Every curse of untimely death that has been taking lives of wives from the hands of their husbands from generation to generation, you have no power over my nieces, I command you to break now by the power in the name of Jesus Christ.

18. Every curse of untimely death that has been taking lives of husbands from the hands of their wives from generation to generation, you have no power over me, I command you to break now by the power in the name of Jesus Christ.

19. Every curse of untimely death that has been taking lives of husbands from the hands of their wives from generation to generation, you have no power over my sons, I command you to break now by the power in the name of Jesus Christ.

20. Every curse of untimely death that has been taking lives of husbands from the hands of their wives from generation to generation, you have no power over my brothers, I command you to break now by the power in the name of Jesus Christ.

21. Every curse of untimely death that has been taking lives of husbands from the hands of their wives from generation to generation, you have no power over my father, I command you to break now by the power in the name of Jesus Christ.
22. Every curse of untimely death that has been taking lives of husbands from the hands of their wives from generation to generation, you have no power over my uncles, I command you to break now by the power in the name of Jesus Christ.
23. Every curse of untimely death that has been taking lives of husbands from the hands of their wives from generation to generation, you have no power over my nephews, I command you to break now by the power in the name of Jesus Christ.
24. Every curse of untimely death that has been taking lives of husbands from the hands of their wives from generation to generation, you have no power over any of my loved ones, I command you to break now by the power in the name of Jesus Christ.
25. Every curse of untimely death that has been taking people's lives before the day of their joy from generation to generation, your assignment is over, I command you to break now over my life in the name of Jesus Christ.
26. Every curse of untimely death that has been taking people's lives before the day of their joy from generation to generation, your assignment is over, I command you to break now over my family in the name of Jesus Christ.
27. Every curse of untimely death that has been taking people's lives before the day of their joy from generation to generation, your assignment is over, I command you

to break now over the life of my spouse in the name of Jesus Christ.
28. Every curse of untimely death that has been taking people's lives before the day of their joy from generation to generation, your assignment is over, I command you to break now over the life of my children in the name of Jesus Christ.
29. Every curse of untimely death that has been taking people's lives before the day of their joy from generation to generation, your assignment is over, I command you to break now over the life of my parents in the name of Jesus Christ.
30. Every curse of untimely death that has been taking people's lives before the day of their joy from generation to generation, your assignment is over, I command you to break now over the life of my siblings in the name of Jesus Christ.
31. Every curse of untimely death that has been taking people's lives before the day of their joy from generation to generation, your assignment is over, I command you to break now over the life of everyone around me in the name of Jesus Christ.
32. Every curse of untimely death that has been taking lives of men from generation to generation and causing children to be left fatherless, I cancel your assignment over family today, I command you to break now by the power in the name of Jesus Christ.
33. Every curse of untimely death that has been taking lives of men from generation to generation and causing children to be left fatherless, I cancel your assignment over my life today, I command you to break now by the power in the name of Jesus Christ.

34. Every curse of untimely death that has been taking lives of men from generation to generation and causing children to be left fatherless, I cancel your assignment over my spouse today, I command you to break now by the power in the name of Jesus Christ.
35. Every curse of untimely death that has been taking lives of men from generation to generation and causing children to be left fatherless, I cancel your assignment over my marriage today, I command you to break now by the power in the name of Jesus Christ.
36. Every curse of untimely death that has been taking lives of men from generation to generation and causing children to be left fatherless, I cancel your assignment over children today, I command you to break now by the power in the name of Jesus Christ.
37. Every curse of untimely death that has been taking lives of women from generation to generation and causing their children to be left motherless, I cancel your assignment over family today, I command you to break now by the power in the name of Jesus Christ.
38. Every curse of untimely death that has been taking lives of women from generation to generation and causing their children to be left motherless, I cancel your assignment over my life today, I command you to break now by the power in the name of Jesus Christ.
39. Every curse of untimely death that has been taking lives of women from generation to generation and causing their children to be left motherless, I cancel your assignment over my spouse today, I command you to break now by the power in the name of Jesus Christ.
40. Every curse of untimely death that has been taking lives of women from generation to generation and causing

their children to be left motherless, I cancel your assignment over my marriage today, I command you to break now by the power in the name of Jesus Christ.

41. Every curse of untimely death that has been taking lives of women from generation to generation and causing their children to be left motherless, I cancel your assignment over my children today, I command you to break now by the power in the name of Jesus Christ.

42. Every curse of untimely death causing people to be lonely, I am not your candidate, I command you to break now by the power in the name of Jesus Christ.

43. Every curse of untimely death causing people to be lonely, my spouse is not your candidate, I command you to break now by the power in the name of Jesus Christ.

44. Every curse of untimely death causing people to be lonely, my children are not your candidate, I command you to break now by the power in the name of Jesus Christ.

DAY FOUR

BREAKING CYCLE OF SUDDEN DEATH

Passages To Read Before You Pray:
Isaiah 10:27, Revelation 12:11, Psalms 3, 35, 70, 88, 140, 83

I stand on the word of God to claim my right as a child of the Kingdom, I cover myself in the blood of Jesus Christ, I cover my household and everything concerning me in the blood of Jesus Christ. I hereby charge this atmosphere by the blood of Jesus Christ and by the fire of the Holy Ghost. I command fresh fire of God to rest upon me now as in the day of Pentecost, let fresh anointing and new oil be released upon me now as I pray. I receive power and authority over the power and the kingdom of darkness, to root out and to pull down, to destroy and to throw down, to build and to plant; whatever I decree in this prayer shall be established; whatever I bind today shall be bound in heaven and whatever I loose today shall be loosed in heaven as it is written in the word of God. Let fresh fire of God be released on my prayer altar and my prayer life now, prince of Persia cannot hinder my prayer, territorial spirit of my neighborhood cannot hinder my prayer, household wickedness cannot hinder my prayer.

I can see my prayer attracting divine intervention. This is the day that the Lord has made, I will rejoice and be glad in it. This is the day that the Lord has chosen to set me free from any form of bondage and break any form of curses upon my life; this is the day that I will receive a total and complete deliverance in every area of my life, today shall mark the beginning of a new thing in my life.

I am a child of God, born of the Spirit, redeemed by the blood of the Lamb. It is written concerning me that power and authority is given unto me over all devils and to cure diseases, I hereby take authority over any form of curses upon my life, be it ancestral, be it generational, be it demon-inflicted or self-inflicted; I command all curses upon my life to break now by the authority in the name of Jesus Christ. The Bible says, where the word of a king is, there is power; today I speak as a king with the authority and power of the King of kings, and I command every other power to bow in the name of Jesus Christ. I render any power behind any curse upon my life useless and ineffective; I overcome any form of distraction, spiritual laziness and slumber, before the end of this prayer session my testimonies shall manifest without delay by the power in the name of Jesus Christ. Amen!

PRAYER POINTS

1. O God my Father, thank you for being my God, my Father and my friend.
2. O God my Father, thank you for the privilege to know you and the power of the resurrection of Jesus Christ.
3. O God my Father, thank you for always being there for me and with me.
4. O God my Father, thank you for the great and mighty things that you are doing in my life.

5. O God my Father, thank you for your provision and protection over me and my household.
6. O God my Father, thank you for always answering my prayers.
7. I confess my sins before you today and I ask you to forgive me on the basis of your mercy, in the name of Jesus Christ.
8. Wash me clean today O Lord by the blood of Jesus Christ.
9. I cover myself and my household with the blood of Jesus Christ.
10. My prayers today will not go in vain; my prayers will produce the desired results in the name of Jesus Christ.
11. Every curse of untimely death that turns laughter to tears, I am not your candidate, I command you to break now by the power in the name of Jesus Christ.
12. Every curse of untimely death that turns laughter to tears, my spouse is not your candidate, I command you to break now by the power in the name of Jesus Christ.
13. Every curse of untimely death that turns laughter to tears, my children are not your candidate, I command you to break now by the power in the name of Jesus Christ.
14. Today I decree by the power and authority in the blood of Jesus Christ, there shall be no sorrow in my home, in the name of Jesus Christ.
15. Today I decree by the power and authority in the blood of Jesus Christ, there shall be no sorrow in my family, in the name of Jesus Christ.
16. Today I decree by the power and authority in the blood of Jesus Christ, there shall be no sorrow concerning my spouse, in the name of Jesus Christ.

17. Today I decree by the power and authority in the blood of Jesus Christ, there shall be no sorrow concerning my children, in the name of Jesus Christ.
18. Today I decree by the power and authority in the blood of Jesus Christ, there shall be no sorrow concerning my parents, in the name of Jesus Christ.
19. Today I decree by the power and authority in the blood of Jesus Christ, there shall be no sorrow concerning my life, in the name of Jesus Christ.
20. Today I decree by the power and authority in the blood of Jesus Christ, there shall be no sorrow in any area of my interest, in the name of Jesus Christ.
21. Today I decree by the power and authority in the blood of Jesus Christ, there shall be no evil report in my home, in the name of Jesus Christ.
22. Today I decree by the power and authority in the blood of Jesus Christ, there shall be no evil report in my family, in the name of Jesus Christ.
23. Today I decree by the power and authority in the blood of Jesus Christ, there shall be no evil report in my marriage, in the name of Jesus Christ.
24. Today I decree by the power and authority in the blood of Jesus Christ, there shall be no evil report concerning my spouse, in the name of Jesus Christ.
25. Today I decree by the power and authority in the blood of Jesus Christ, there shall be no evil report concerning my children, in the name of Jesus Christ.
26. Today I decree by the power and authority in the blood of Jesus Christ, there shall be no evil report concerning my parents, in the name of Jesus Christ.

27. Today I decree by the power and authority in the blood of Jesus Christ, there shall be no evil report concerning my life, in the name of Jesus Christ.
28. Today I decree by the power and authority in the blood of Jesus Christ, there shall be no evil report concerning my business, in the name of Jesus Christ.
29. Today I decree by the power and authority in the blood of Jesus Christ, there shall be no evil report in any area of my interest, in the name of Jesus Christ.
30. Today I decree by the power and authority in the blood of Jesus Christ that the noise of crying and wailing shall not be heard in my house, in the name of Jesus Christ.
31. Every cycle of untimely death in my life, enough is enough, I command you to break now by the power in the name of Jesus Christ.
32. Every cycle of untimely death in my family, enough is enough, I command you to break now by the power in the name of Jesus Christ.
33. Every cycle of untimely death affecting the life of my spouse, enough is enough, I command you to break now by the power in the name of Jesus Christ.
34. Every cycle of untimely death affecting the life of my children, enough is enough, I command you to break now by the power in the name of Jesus Christ.
35. Every cycle of untimely death in the life of my parents, enough of enough, I command you to break now by the power in the name of Jesus Christ.
36. Every cycle of untimely death affecting my progress, enough is enough, I command you to break now by the power in the name of Jesus Christ.

37. Every cycle of untimely death affecting my fruitfulness, enough is enough, I command you to break now by the power in the name of Jesus Christ.
38. Every cycle of untimely death causing me to live a roller-coaster life, enough is enough, I command you to break right now by the power in the name of Jesus Christ.
39. O God my Father, let season of sorrow end now and let season of rejoicing begin, in the name of Jesus Christ.
40. O God my Father, let season of tragedy end now and let season of celebration begin, in the name of Jesus Christ.
41. O God my Father, let season of weeping end now and let season of laughter begin, in the name of Jesus Christ.
42. Today I decree that the joy of the Lord shall be strength in the name of Jesus Christ.

DAY FIVE

I SHALL NOT DIE BUT LIVE

Passages To Read Before You Pray:
Ezekiel 37:1-10, Psalms 22, 10, 118, 55, 109, 91, 68

I stand on the word of God to claim my right as a child of the Kingdom, I cover myself in the blood of Jesus Christ, I cover my household and everything concerning me in the blood of Jesus Christ. I hereby charge this atmosphere by the blood of Jesus Christ and by the fire of the Holy Ghost. I command fresh fire of God to rest upon me now as in the day of Pentecost, let fresh anointing and new oil be released upon me now as I pray. I receive power and authority over the power and the kingdom of darkness, to root out and to pull down, to destroy and to throw down, to build and to plant; whatever I decree in this prayer shall be established; whatever I bind today shall be bound in heaven and whatever I loose today shall be loosed in heaven as it is written in the word of God. Let fresh fire of God be released on my prayer altar and my prayer life now, prince of Persia cannot hinder my prayer, territorial spirit of my neighborhood cannot hinder my prayer, household wickedness cannot hinder my prayer.

I can see my prayer attracting divine intervention. This is the day that the Lord has made, I will rejoice and be glad in it. This is the day that the Lord has chosen to set me free from any form of

bondage and break any form of curses upon my life; this is the day that I will receive a total and complete deliverance in every area of my life, today shall mark the beginning of a new thing in my life.

I am a child of God, born of the Spirit, redeemed by the blood of the Lamb. It is written concerning me that power and authority is given unto me over all devils and to cure diseases, I hereby take authority over any form of curses upon my life, be it ancestral, be it generational, be it demon-inflicted or self-inflicted; I command all curses upon my life to break now by the authority in the name of Jesus Christ. The Bible says, where the word of a king is, there is power; today I speak as a king with the authority and power of the King of kings, and I command every other power to bow in the name of Jesus Christ. I render any power behind any curse upon my life useless and ineffective; I overcome any form of distraction, spiritual laziness and slumber, before the end of this prayer session my testimonies shall manifest without delay by the power in the name of Jesus Christ. Amen!

PRAYER POINTS

1. O God my Father, thank you for being my God, my Father and my friend.
2. O God my Father, thank you for the privilege to know you and the power of the resurrection of Jesus Christ.
3. O God my Father, thank you for always being there for me and with me.
4. O God my Father, thank you for the great and mighty things that you are doing in my life.

5. O God my Father, thank you for your provision and protection over me and my household.
6. O God my Father, thank you for always answering my prayers.
7. I confess my sins before you today and I ask you to forgive me on the basis of your mercy, in the name of Jesus Christ.
8. Wash me clean today O Lord by the blood of Jesus Christ.
9. I cover myself and my household with the blood of Jesus Christ.
10. My prayers today will not go in vain; my prayers will produce the desired results in the name of Jesus Christ.
11. This year and all the days of my life, I shall have no reason to cry in the name of Jesus Christ.
12. My God is doing new things in my life, therefore I will laugh a new laugh, dance a new dance, sing a new song, and everyone around me will celebrate with me in the name of Jesus Christ.
13. Any covenant binding me with the curse of untimely death, I command you to break now by the power in the name of Jesus Christ.
14. Any covenant binding my spouse with the curse of untimely death, I command you to break now by the power in the name of Jesus Christ.
15. Any covenant binding my children with the curse of untimely death, I command you to break now by the power in the name of Jesus Christ.
16. Any covenant binding any member of my family with the curse of untimely death, I command you to break now by the power in the name of Jesus Christ.

17. Every power of the grave assigned to take me early, you are a liar, I am not your candidate, I command you to loose your hold over my life in the name of Jesus Christ.
18. Every power of the grave assigned to take my spouse early, you are a liar, my spouse is not your candidate, I command you to loose your hold over the life of my spouse now in the name of Jesus Christ.
19. Every power of the grave assigned to take my children early, you are a liar, my children are not your candidate, I command you to loose your hold over the life of my children now, in the name of Jesus Christ.
20. Every power of the grave assigned to take any of my loved ones early, you are a liar, my loved ones are not your candidate, I command you to loose your hold over my family and loved ones now, in the name of Jesus Christ.
21. Every strongman of untimely death that has been working against my lineage from generation to generation, you are no longer allowed to do so in the name of Jesus Christ.
22. Every strongman of untimely death that has been working my bloodline, I command you to stop today by the power and authority in the name of Jesus Christ.
23. Every strongman of untimely death that has been killing people from generation to generation in my lineage, you have no power over me, I destroy all your plans concerning my life in the name of Jesus Christ.
24. Every strongman of untimely death that has been killing people from generation to generation in my lineage, you have no power over my spouse, I destroy all your plans concerning my spouse in the name of Jesus Christ.

25. Every strongman of untimely death that has been killing people from generation to generation in my lineage, you have no power over my children, I destroy all your plans concerning the lives of my children in the name of Jesus Christ.
26. Every strongman of untimely death that has been killing people from generation to generation in my lineage, you have no power over my future generations, I destroy all your plans concerning my future generations in the name of Jesus Christ.
27. Ancestral voice of death calling me from the grave, I command you to be silenced forever, in the name of Jesus Christ.
28. Ancestral voice of death calling my spouse from the grave, I command you to be silenced forever, in the name of Jesus Christ.
29. Ancestral voice of death calling any of my children from the grave, I command you to be silenced forever, in the name of Jesus Christ.
30. Every strongman of death assigned to kill me before my time, you will not escape the judgment of God, in the name of Jesus Christ.
31. Every strongman of death assigned to kill my spouse before his/her time, you will not escape the judgment of God, in the name of Jesus Christ.
32. Every strongman of death assigned to kill my children before their time, you will not escape the judgment of God, in the name of Jesus Christ.
33. Any power anywhere assigned to pursue me to untimely grave, I arrest you today and send you back to the pit of hell, in the name of Jesus Christ.

34. Any power anywhere assigned to pursue my spouse to untimely grave, I arrest you today and send you back to the pit of hell, in the name of Jesus Christ.
35. Any power anywhere assigned to pursue my children to untimely grave, I arrest you today and send you back to the pit of hell, in the name of Jesus Christ.
36. Any power anywhere assigned to pursue any member of my family to untimely grave, I arrest you today and send you back to the pit of hell, in the name of Jesus Christ.
37. O God my Father, redeem my life from the power of the grave according to your word, in the name of Jesus Christ.
38. O God my Father, redeem my spouse from the power of the grave according to your word, in the name of Jesus Christ.
39. O God my Father, redeem my children from the power of the grave according to your word, in the name of Jesus Christ.
40. It is written concerning me, I will not die but live to declare the works of God, in the name of Jesus Christ.
41. It is written in the word, my spouse will not die but live to declare the works of God, in the name of Jesus Christ.
42. It is written in the word, my children will not die but live to declare the works of God, in the name of Jesus Christ.
43. Every chain of untimely death in my family, I command you to break now by the power in the name of Jesus Christ.

DELIVERANCE FROM FRUSTRATIONS

(5 DAYS FASTING & INTENSIVE PRAYER)

KEY BIBLE PASSAGE

"Thus saith the Lord GOD; Remove the diadem, and take off the crown: this shall not be the same: exalt him that is low, and abase him that is high. I will overturn, overturn, overturn, it: and it shall be no more, until he come whose right it is; and I will give it him." – Ezekiel 21:26-27

DAY ONE

GENERATIONAL REPENTANCE

Passages To Read Before You Pray:
Exodus 20:1-5, Jeremiah 31:27-34, Daniel 9:1-19, Psalms 89

I stand on the word of God to claim my right as a child of the Kingdom, I cover myself in the blood of Jesus Christ, I cover my household and everything concerning me in the blood of Jesus Christ. I hereby charge this atmosphere by the blood of Jesus Christ and by the fire of the Holy Ghost. I command fresh fire of God to rest upon me now as in the day of Pentecost, let fresh anointing and new oil be released upon me now as I pray. I receive power and authority over the power and the kingdom of darkness, to root out and to pull down, to destroy and to throw down, to build and to plant; whatever I decree in this prayer shall be established; whatever I bind today shall be bound in heaven and whatever I loose today shall be loosed in heaven as it is written in the word of God. Let fresh fire of God be released on my prayer altar and my prayer life now, prince of Persia cannot hinder my prayer, territorial spirit of my neighborhood cannot hinder my prayer, household wickedness cannot hinder my prayer.

I can see my prayer attracting divine intervention. This is the day that the Lord has made, I will rejoice and be glad in it. This is the day that the Lord has chosen to set me free from any form of

bondage and break any form of curses upon my life; this is the day that I will receive a total and complete deliverance in every area of my life, today shall mark the beginning of a new thing in my life.

I am a child of God, born of the Spirit, redeemed by the blood of the Lamb. It is written concerning me that power and authority is given unto me over all devils and to cure diseases, I hereby take authority over any form of curses upon my life, be it ancestral, be it generational, be it demon-inflicted or self-inflicted; I command all curses upon my life to break now by the authority in the name of Jesus Christ. The Bible says, where the word of a king is, there is power; today I speak as a king with the authority and power of the King of kings, and I command every other power to bow in the name of Jesus Christ. I render any power behind any curse upon my life useless and ineffective; I overcome any form of distraction, spiritual laziness and slumber, before the end of this prayer session my testimonies shall manifest without delay by the power in the name of Jesus Christ. Amen!

PRAYER POINTS

1. God my Father, thank you for being my God, my Father and my friend.
2. God my Father, thank you for the privilege to know you and the power of the resurrection of Jesus Christ.
3. God my Father, thank you for always being there for me and with me.
4. God my Father, thank you for the great and mighty things that you are doing in my life.

5. God my Father, thank you for your provision and protection over me and my household.
6. God my Father, thank you for always answering my prayers.
7. God my Father, I confess and repent of all sins in my life or my ancestors' lives that have resulted in a curse upon my life or bloodline; forgive me Lord on the basis of your mercy and cleanse me by the blood of Jesus Christ.
8. God my Father, I confess today and repent of all sins of disobedience in my life or my ancestor's lives that have resulted in a curse upon my life or bloodline; forgive me Lord on the basis of your mercy and cleanse me by the blood of Jesus Christ.
9. God my Father, I confess today and repent of all sins of rebellion in my life or my ancestor's lives that have resulted in a curse upon my life or bloodline; forgive me Lord on the basis of your mercy and cleanse me by the blood of Jesus Christ.
10. God my Father, I confess today and repent of all sins of perversion in my life or my ancestor's lives that have resulted in a curse upon my life or bloodline; forgive me Lord on the basis of your mercy and cleanse me by the blood of Jesus Christ.
11. God my Father, I confess today and repent of all sins of witchcraft in my life or my ancestor's lives that have resulted in a curse upon my life or bloodline; forgive me Lord on the basis of your mercy and cleanse me by the blood of Jesus Christ.
12. God my Father, I confess today and repent of all sins of idolatry in my life or my ancestor's lives that have resulted in a curse upon my life or bloodline; forgive

me Lord on the basis of your mercy and cleanse me by the blood of Jesus Christ.

13. God my Father, I confess today and repent of all sins of lust in my life or my ancestor's lives that have resulted in a curse upon my life or bloodline; forgive me Lord on the basis of your mercy and cleanse me by the blood of Jesus Christ.

14. God my Father, I confess today and repent of all sins of adultery in my life or my ancestor's lives that have resulted in a curse upon my life or bloodline; forgive me Lord on the basis of your mercy and cleanse me by the blood of Jesus Christ.

15. God my Father, I confess today and repent of all sins of fornication in my life or my ancestor's lives that have resulted in a curse upon my life or bloodline; forgive me Lord on the basis of your mercy and cleanse me by the blood of Jesus Christ.

16. God my Father, I confess today and repent of all sins of mistreatment of others in my life or my ancestor's lives that have resulted in a curse upon my life or bloodline; forgive me Lord on the basis of your mercy and cleanse me by the blood of Jesus Christ.

17. God my Father, I confess today and repent of all sins of murder or abortion in my life or my ancestor's lives that have resulted in a curse upon my life or bloodline; forgive me Lord on the basis of your mercy and cleanse me by the blood of Jesus Christ.

18. God my Father, I confess today and repent of all sins of cheating in my life or my ancestor's lives that have resulted in a curse upon my life or bloodline; forgive me Lord on the basis of your mercy and cleanse me by the blood of Jesus Christ.

19. God my Father, I confess today and repent of all sins of lying in my life or my ancestor's lives that have resulted in a curse upon my life or bloodline; forgive me Lord on the basis of your mercy and cleanse me by the blood of Jesus Christ.
20. God my Father, I confess today and repent of all sins of sorcery in my life or my ancestor's lives that have resulted in a curse upon my life or bloodline; forgive me Lord on the basis of your mercy and cleanse me by the blood of Jesus Christ.
21. God my Father, I confess today and repent of all sins of divination in my life or my ancestor's lives that have resulted in a curse upon my life or bloodline; forgive me Lord on the basis of your mercy and cleanse me by the blood of Jesus Christ.
22. God my Father, I confess today and repent of all sins of occult involvement in my life or my ancestor's lives that have resulted in a curse upon my life or bloodline; forgive me Lord on the basis of your mercy and cleanse me by the blood of Jesus Christ.
23. I disassociate myself from all evil done by my ancestors by the power in the blood of Jesus Christ.
24. I disassociate myself from all evil attitudes done by my ancestors against the will and purpose of God, in the name of Jesus Christ.
25. With all my heart I disagree with all sins committed by my ancestors, Father Lord have mercy and cleanse me by the blood of Jesus Christ.
26. Today with all my heart I declare that I refuse to be like my parents, in the name of Jesus Christ.
27. Today with all my heart I declare that I refuse to be like any of my ancestors, in the name of Jesus Christ.

28. I refuse to suffer the same problems as my parents, I reject it; my heart, soul, spirit and body reject it in the name of Jesus Christ.
29. I refuse to suffer the same problems as any of my ancestors, I reject it; my heart, soul, spirit and body reject it in the name of Jesus Christ.
30. In the name of Jesus Christ, I refuse to go through what my parents went through, my case is different, I am a child of God and covered by the blood of Jesus Christ.
31. By the power and authority in the blood of Jesus Christ, I sever myself from my bloodline, in the name of Jesus Christ.
32. By the power and authority in the blood of Jesus Christ, I sever myself from the connection to any of my ancestors, in the name of Jesus Christ.
33. By the power and authority in the blood of Jesus Christ, I sever myself from spiritual connection to any of my ancestors, in the name of Jesus Christ.
34. By the power and authority in the blood of Jesus Christ, I sever myself from physical connection to any of my ancestors, in the name of Jesus Christ.
35. By the power and authority in the blood of Jesus Christ, I sever myself from emotional connection to any of my ancestors, in the name of Jesus Christ.
36. By the power and authority in the blood of Jesus Christ, I sever myself from mental connection to any of my ancestors, in the name of Jesus Christ.
37. By the power and authority in the blood of Jesus Christ, I sever myself from the connection to the idol of my father's house, in the name of Jesus Christ.

38. By the power and authority in the blood of Jesus Christ, I sever myself from the connection to the idol of my mother's house, in the name of Jesus Christ.
39. By the power and authority in the blood of Jesus Christ, I destroy every spiritual DNA that links me to my ancestors by the fire of God, in the name of Jesus Christ.
40. By the power and authority in the blood of Jesus Christ, I destroy every spiritual DNA that links my children to my ancestors by the fire of God, in the name of Jesus Christ.

DAY TWO

DELIVERANCE FROM CURSES OF FRUSTRATION

Passages To Read Before You Pray:
Genesis 11:1-9, Isaiah 47:1-15, Psalms 3, 9, 59, 69, 140, 83

I stand on the word of God to claim my right as a child of the Kingdom, I cover myself in the blood of Jesus Christ, I cover my household and everything concerning me in the blood of Jesus Christ. I hereby charge this atmosphere by the blood of Jesus Christ and by the fire of the Holy Ghost. I command fresh fire of God to rest upon me now as in the day of Pentecost, let fresh anointing and new oil be released upon me now as I pray. I receive power and authority over the power and the kingdom of darkness, to root out and to pull down, to destroy and to throw down, to build and to plant; whatever I decree in this prayer shall be established; whatever I bind today shall be bound in heaven and whatever I loose today shall be loosed in heaven as it is written in the word of God. Let fresh fire of God be released on my prayer altar and my prayer life now, prince of Persia cannot hinder my prayer, territorial spirit of my neighborhood cannot hinder my prayer, household wickedness cannot hinder my prayer.

I can see my prayer attracting divine intervention. This is the day that the Lord has made, I will rejoice and be glad in it. This is the day that the Lord has chosen to set me free from any form of

bondage and break any form of curses upon my life; this is the day that I will receive a total and complete deliverance in every area of my life, today shall mark the beginning of a new thing in my life.

I am a child of God, born of the Spirit, redeemed by the blood of the Lamb. It is written concerning me that power and authority is given unto me over all devils and to cure diseases, I hereby take authority over any form of curses upon my life, be it ancestral, be it generational, be it demon-inflicted or self-inflicted; I command all curses upon my life to break now by the authority in the name of Jesus Christ. The Bible says, where the word of a king is, there is power; today I speak as a king with the authority and power of the King of kings, and I command every other power to bow in the name of Jesus Christ. I render any power behind any curse upon my life useless and ineffective; I overcome any form of distraction, spiritual laziness and slumber, before the end of this prayer session my testimonies shall manifest without delay by the power in the name of Jesus Christ. Amen!

PRAYER POINTS

1. God my Father, thank you for being my God, my Father and my friend.
2. God my Father, thank you for the privilege to know you and the power of the resurrection of Jesus Christ.
3. God my Father, thank you for always being there for me and with me.
4. God my Father, thank you for the great and mighty things that you are doing in my life.

5. God my Father, thank you for your provision and protection over me and my household.
6. God my Father, thank you for always answering my prayers.
7. I confess my sins before you today and I ask you to forgive me on the basis of your mercy, in the name of Jesus Christ.
8. Wash me clean today O Lord by the blood of Jesus Christ.
9. I cover myself and my household with the blood of Jesus Christ.
10. My prayers today will not go in vain; my prayers will produce the desired results in the name of Jesus Christ.
11. By the power and authority in the blood of Jesus Christ, I break every curse of frustration in my bloodline from my life to my past generations all the way to Adam the first man, in the name of Jesus Christ.
12. I take authority and break every curse of frustration over my life by the power in the name of Jesus Christ.
13. I take authority and break every curse of frustration affecting my family, in the name of Jesus Christ.
14. I take authority and break every curse of frustration affecting my spouse, in the name of Jesus Christ.
15. I take authority and break every curse of frustration affecting my children, in the name of Jesus Christ.
16. I take authority and break every curse of frustration affecting my business, in the name of Jesus Christ.
17. I take authority and break every curse of frustration affecting my progress in the name of Jesus Christ.
18. I take authority and break every curse of frustration affecting my marriage, in the name of Jesus Christ.

19. I take authority and break every curse of frustration affecting my relationship, in the name of Jesus Christ.
20. I take authority and break every curse of frustration affecting my relationship with God, in the name of Jesus Christ.
21. I take authority and break every curse of frustration affecting my spiritual growth, in the name of Jesus Christ.
22. I take authority and break every curse of frustration affecting my ministry, in the name of Jesus Christ.
23. I take authority and break every curse of frustration affecting my joy by the power in the name of Jesus Christ.
24. By the power and authority in the blood of Jesus Christ, I break every curse of frustration delaying my breakthrough, in the name of Jesus Christ.
25. By the power and authority in the blood of Jesus Christ, I break every curse of frustration driving my helpers away from me, in the name of Jesus Christ.
26. By the power and authority in the blood of Jesus Christ, I break every curse of frustration blocking my open heavens, in the name of Jesus Christ.
27. By the power and authority in the blood of Jesus Christ, I break every curse of frustration blocking my miracles, in the name of Jesus Christ.
28. By the power and authority in the blood of Jesus Christ, I break every curse of frustration delaying the move of God in my life, in the name of Jesus Christ.
29. By the power and authority in the blood of Jesus Christ, I break every curse of frustration delaying the manifestation of God's power in my life, in the name of Jesus Christ.

30. By the power and authority in the blood of Jesus Christ, I break every curse of frustration hindering my financial freedom, in the name of Jesus Christ.
31. By the power and authority in the blood of Jesus Christ, I break every curse of frustration that has been holding my life back, in the name of Jesus Christ.
32. By the power and authority in the blood of Jesus Christ, I break every power of inherited frustration over my life, in the name of Jesus Christ.
33. By the power and authority in the blood of Jesus Christ, I break every power of inherited frustration over my family, in the name of Jesus Christ.
34. By the power and authority in the blood of Jesus Christ, I break every inherited frustration over my marriage, in the name of Jesus Christ.
35. By the power and authority in the blood of Jesus Christ, I break every power of inherited frustration over the life of my spouse, in the name of Jesus Christ.
36. By the power and authority in the blood of Jesus Christ, I break every power of inherited frustration over the life of my children, in the name of Jesus Christ.
37. By the power and authority in the blood of Jesus Christ, I break every power of inherited frustration over my future generations, in the name of Jesus Christ.

DAY THREE

PRAYER TO STOP ANCESTRAL EVIL FLOW

Passages To Read Before You Pray:
Jeremiah 31:27-32, Job 22:28, Psalms 30, 34, 38, 107, 70, 86

I stand on the word of God to claim my right as a child of the Kingdom, I cover myself in the blood of Jesus Christ, I cover my household and everything concerning me in the blood of Jesus Christ. I hereby charge this atmosphere by the blood of Jesus Christ and by the fire of the Holy Ghost. I command fresh fire of God to rest upon me now as in the day of Pentecost, let fresh anointing and new oil be released upon me now as I pray. I receive power and authority over the power and the kingdom of darkness, to root out and to pull down, to destroy and to throw down, to build and to plant; whatever I decree in this prayer shall be established; whatever I bind today shall be bound in heaven and whatever I loose today shall be loosed in heaven as it is written in the word of God. Let fresh fire of God be released on my prayer altar and my prayer life now, prince of Persia cannot hinder my prayer, territorial spirit of my neighborhood cannot hinder my prayer, household wickedness cannot hinder my prayer.

I can see my prayer attracting divine intervention. This is the day that the Lord has made, I will rejoice and be glad in it. This is the day that the Lord has chosen to set me free from any form of

bondage and break any form of curses upon my life; this is the day that I will receive a total and complete deliverance in every area of my life, today shall mark the beginning of a new thing in my life.

I am a child of God, born of the Spirit, redeemed by the blood of the Lamb. It is written concerning me that power and authority is given unto me over all devils and to cure diseases, I hereby take authority over any form of curses upon my life, be it ancestral, be it generational, be it demon-inflicted or self-inflicted; I command all curses upon my life to break now by the authority in the name of Jesus Christ. The Bible says, where the word of a king is, there is power; today I speak as a king with the authority and power of the King of kings, and I command every other power to bow in the name of Jesus Christ. I render any power behind any curse upon my life useless and ineffective; I overcome any form of distraction, spiritual laziness and slumber, before the end of this prayer session my testimonies shall manifest without delay by the power in the name of Jesus Christ. Amen!

PRAYER POINTS

1. O God my Father, thank you for being my God, my Father and my friend.
2. O God my Father, thank you for the privilege to know you and the power of the resurrection of Jesus Christ.
3. O God my Father, thank you for always being there for me and with me.
4. O God my Father, thank you for the great and mighty things that you are doing in my life.

5. O God my Father, thank you for your provision and protection over me and my household.
6. O God my Father, thank you for always answering my prayers.
7. I confess my sins before you today and I ask you to forgive me on the basis of your mercy, in the name of Jesus Christ.
8. Wash me clean today O Lord by the blood of Jesus Christ.
9. I cover myself and my household with the blood of Jesus Christ.
10. My prayers today will not go in vain; my prayers will produce the desired results in the name of Jesus Christ.
11. Ancestral flow of frustration upon my life, I command you to stop now by the power in the name of Jesus Christ.
12. Ancestral flow of frustration upon my family, I command you to stop now by the power in the name of Jesus Christ.
13. Ancestral flow of frustration affecting my marriage, I command you to stop now by the power in the name of Jesus Christ.
14. Ancestral flow of frustration upon the life of my spouse, I command you to stop now by the power in the name of Jesus Christ.
15. Ancestral flow of frustration upon the life of my children, I command you to stop now by the power in the name of Jesus Christ.
16. Ancestral flow of frustration upon the life of my parents, I command you to stop now by the power in the name of Jesus Christ.

17. Ancestral flow of frustration affecting my business, I command you to stop now by the power in the name of Jesus Christ.
18. Ancestral flow of frustration upon my labor, I command you to stop now by the power in the name of Jesus Christ.
19. Ancestral flow of frustration affecting my finances, I command you to stop now by the power in the name of Jesus Christ.
20. Ancestral flow of frustration affecting the works of my hands, I command you to stop now by the power in the name of Jesus Christ.
21. Ancestral flow of frustration upon my destiny, I command you to stop now by the power in the name of Jesus Christ.
22. Ancestral flow of frustration upon my future, I command you to stop now by the power in the name of Jesus Christ.
23. Ancestral flow of frustration upon every area of my life, I command you to stop now by the power in the name of Jesus Christ.
24. Ancestral flow of frustration upon every stage of my life, I command you to stop now by the power in the name of Jesus Christ.
25. Every challenge causing frustration in my life, I command you to receive permanent solution now in the name of Jesus Christ.
26. Every spiritual challenge causing frustration in my life, I command you to receive permanent solution now, in the name of Jesus Christ.

27. Every financial challenge causing frustration in my life, I command you to receive permanent solution now in the name of Jesus Christ.
28. Every academic challenge causing frustration in my life, I command you to receive permanent solution now, in the name of Jesus Christ.
29. Every challenge that I encounter at work causing frustration in my life, I command you to receive permanent solution now in the name of Jesus Christ.
30. Every curse of frustration causing me to have all kinds of mental struggles, I command you to break now by the power in the name of Jesus Christ.
31. Every curse of frustration causing me to have all kinds of financial struggles, I command you to break now by the power in the name of Jesus Christ.
32. Every satanic agent assigned to frustrate my life, I bind you and command you to loose your hold over my life, in the name of Jesus Christ.
33. Every satanic agent assigned to frustrate my family, I bind you and command you to loose your hold over my family, in the name of Jesus Christ.
34. You spirit of frustration, I rebuke you in the name of Jesus Christ, you cannot do what you did to my parents to me, my case is different.
35. You spirit of frustration, I rebuke you in the name of Jesus Christ, you cannot do what you did to my parents to my children, this case is different.
36. You spirit of frustration, I rebuke you in the name of Jesus Christ, you cannot do what you did to my parents to my children's children, this case is different.

37. You spirit of frustration, I rebuke you in the name of Jesus Christ, you cannot do what you did to my parents to my spouse, this case is different.
38. You spirit of frustration, I rebuke you in the name of Jesus Christ, you cannot do what you did to my ancestors to me, my case is different.

DAY FOUR

PRAYER FOR SUPERNATURAL TURN-AROUND

Passages To Read Before You Pray:
1 Chronicles 4:9-10, Ezekiel 21:26-27, Habakkuk 1:5, Psalms 9, 35, 70, 68, 83

I stand on the word of God to claim my right as a child of the Kingdom, I cover myself in the blood of Jesus Christ, I cover my household and everything concerning me in the blood of Jesus Christ. I hereby charge this atmosphere by the blood of Jesus Christ and by the fire of the Holy Ghost. I command fresh fire of God to rest upon me now as in the day of Pentecost, let fresh anointing and new oil be released upon me now as I pray. I receive power and authority over the power and the kingdom of darkness, to root out and to pull down, to destroy and to throw down, to build and to plant; whatever I decree in this prayer shall be established; whatever I bind today shall be bound in heaven and whatever I loose today shall be loosed in heaven as it is written in the word of God. Let fresh fire of God be released on my prayer altar and my prayer life now, prince of Persia cannot hinder my prayer, territorial spirit of my neighborhood cannot hinder my prayer, household wickedness cannot hinder my prayer.

I can see my prayer attracting divine intervention. This is the day that the Lord has made, I will rejoice and be glad in it. This is the

day that the Lord has chosen to set me free from any form of bondage and break any form of curses upon my life; this is the day that I will receive a total and complete deliverance in every area of my life, today shall mark the beginning of a new thing in my life.

I am a child of God, born of the Spirit, redeemed by the blood of the Lamb. It is written concerning me that power and authority is given unto me over all devils and to cure diseases, I hereby take authority over any form of curses upon my life, be it ancestral, be it generational, be it demon-inflicted or self-inflicted; I command all curses upon my life to break now by the authority in the name of Jesus Christ. The Bible says, where the word of a king is, there is power; today I speak as a king with the authority and power of the King of kings, and I command every other power to bow in the name of Jesus Christ. I render any power behind any curse upon my life useless and ineffective; I overcome any form of distraction, spiritual laziness and slumber, before the end of this prayer session my testimonies shall manifest without delay by the power in the name of Jesus Christ. Amen!

PRAYER POINTS

1. O God my Father, thank you for being my God, my Father and my friend.
2. O God my Father, thank you for the privilege to know you and the power of the resurrection of Jesus Christ.
3. O God my Father, thank you for always being there for me and with me.

4. O God my Father, thank you for the great and mighty things that you are doing in my life.
5. O God my Father, thank you for your provision and protection over me and my household.
6. O God my Father, thank you for always answering my prayers.
7. I confess my sins before you today and I ask you to forgive me on the basis of your mercy, in the name of Jesus Christ.
8. Wash me clean today O Lord by the blood of Jesus Christ.
9. I cover myself and my household with the blood of Jesus Christ.
10. My prayers today will not go in vain; my prayers will produce the desired results in the name of Jesus Christ.
11. I stand upon the Word of God and decree that every situation of life causing me to be frustrated receive a positive turn around today, in the name of Jesus Christ.
12. I stand upon the Word of God and decree that every situation of life causing my family to be frustrated receive a positive turn around today, in the name of Jesus Christ.
13. I stand upon the Word of God and decree that every situation of life causing my marriage to be frustrated receive a positive turn around today, in the name of Jesus Christ.
14. I stand upon the Word of God and decree that every situation of life causing my ministry to be frustrated receive a positive turn around today, in the name of Jesus Christ.
15. I stand upon the Word of God and decree that every situation of life causing my business to be frustrated

receive a positive turn around today, in the name of Jesus Christ.
16. I stand upon the Word of God and decree that every situation of life causing my spouse to be frustrated receive a positive turn around today, in the name of Jesus Christ.
17. I stand upon the Word of God and decree that every situation of life causing my children to be frustrated receive a positive turn around today, in the name of Jesus Christ.
18. I stand upon the Word of God and decree that every situation of life causing my parents to be frustrated receive a positive turn around today, in the name of Jesus Christ.
19. I stand upon the Word of God and decree that every situation of life causing my breakthrough to be frustrated receive a positive turn around today, in the name of Jesus Christ.
20. I stand upon the Word of God and decree by the authority in the name of Jesus Christ, no more frustration, I receive the anointing for financial breakthrough today.
21. I stand upon the Word of God and decree by the authority in the name of Jesus Christ, no more frustration, I receive the anointing for double promotion today.
22. I stand upon the Word of God and decree by the authority in the name of Jesus Christ, no more frustration, I receive the anointing for uncommon favor today.
23. I stand upon the Word of God and decree by the authority in the name of Jesus Christ, no more

frustration, I receive the anointing for uncommon victory today.
24. I stand upon the Word of God and decree by the authority in the name of Jesus Christ, no more frustration, I receive the anointing for supernatural turn-around today.
25. I stand upon the Word of God and decree by the authority in the name of Jesus Christ, no more frustration, I receive the anointing for unbelievable miracles today.
26. I stand upon the Word of God and decree by the authority in the name of Jesus Christ, no more frustration, I receive the anointing for unstoppable progress today.
27. I stand upon the Word of God and decree by the authority in the name of Jesus Christ, no more frustration, I receive the anointing for open heavens today.
28. I stand upon the Word of God and decree by the authority in the name of Jesus Christ, no more frustration, I receive the anointing for answered prayers today.
29. I stand upon the Word of God and decree by the authority in the name of Jesus Christ, no more frustration, I receive the anointing for open doors today.
30. I stand upon the Word of God and decree by the authority in the name of Jesus Christ, no more frustration, I receive the anointing for divine connections today.
31. I stand upon the Word of God and decree by the authority in the name of Jesus Christ, no more

frustration, I receive the anointing for divine healing today.

32. I stand upon the Word of God and decree by the authority in the name of Jesus Christ, no more frustration, I receive the anointing for total deliverance today.

33. I stand upon the Word of God and decree by the authority in the name of Jesus Christ, no more frustration, I receive the anointing for uncommon increase today.

34. I stand upon the Word of God and decree by the authority in the name of Jesus Christ, no more frustration, I receive the anointing for abundance today.

35. I stand upon the Word of God and decree by the authority in the name of Jesus Christ, no more frustration, I receive the anointing for restoration today.

36. I stand upon the Word of God and decree by the authority in the name of Jesus Christ, no more frustration, I receive the anointing for financial success today.

37. I stand upon the Word of God and decree by the authority in the name of Jesus Christ, no more frustration, I receive the anointing for business success today.

DAY FIVE

NO MORE FRUSTRATION

Passages To Read Before You Pray:
Isaiah 41:10-13, Revelation 21:4, Psalms 34, 27, 42, 19, 105

I stand on the word of God to claim my right as a child of the Kingdom, I cover myself in the blood of Jesus Christ, I cover my household and everything concerning me in the blood of Jesus Christ. I hereby charge this atmosphere by the blood of Jesus Christ and by the fire of the Holy Ghost. I command fresh fire of God to rest upon me now as in the day of Pentecost, let fresh anointing and new oil be released upon me now as I pray. I receive power and authority over the power and the kingdom of darkness, to root out and to pull down, to destroy and to throw down, to build and to plant; whatever I decree in this prayer shall be established; whatever I bind today shall be bound in heaven and whatever I loose today shall be loosed in heaven as it is written in the word of God. Let fresh fire of God be released on my prayer altar and my prayer life now, prince of Persia cannot hinder my prayer, territorial spirit of my neighborhood cannot hinder my prayer, household wickedness cannot hinder my prayer.

I can see my prayer attracting divine intervention. This is the day that the Lord has made, I will rejoice and be glad in it. This is the day that the Lord has chosen to set me free from any form of

bondage and break any form of curses upon my life; this is the day that I will receive a total and complete deliverance in every area of my life, today shall mark the beginning of a new thing in my life.

I am a child of God, born of the Spirit, redeemed by the blood of the Lamb. It is written concerning me that power and authority is given unto me over all devils and to cure diseases, I hereby take authority over any form of curses upon my life, be it ancestral, be it generational, be it demon-inflicted or self-inflicted; I command all curses upon my life to break now by the authority in the name of Jesus Christ. The Bible says, where the word of a king is, there is power; today I speak as a king with the authority and power of the King of kings, and I command every other power to bow in the name of Jesus Christ. I render any power behind any curse upon my life useless and ineffective; I overcome any form of distraction, spiritual laziness and slumber, before the end of this prayer session my testimonies shall manifest without delay by the power in the name of Jesus Christ. Amen!

PRAYER POINTS

1. O God my Father, thank you for being my God, my Father and my friend.
2. O God my Father, thank you for the privilege to know you and the power of the resurrection of Jesus Christ.
3. O God my Father, thank you for always being there for me and with me.
4. O God my Father, thank you for the great and mighty things that you are doing in my life.

5. O God my Father, thank you for your provision and protection over me and my household.
6. O God my Father, thank you for always answering my prayers.
7. I confess my sins before you today and I ask you to forgive me on the basis of your mercy, in the name of Jesus Christ.
8. Wash me clean today O Lord by the blood of Jesus Christ.
9. I cover myself and my household with the blood of Jesus Christ.
10. My prayers today will not go in vain; my prayers will produce the desired results in the name of Jesus Christ.
11. I stand upon the Word of God and decree by the authority in the name of Jesus Christ, no more frustration, I receive the anointing for academic success today.
12. I stand upon the Word of God and decree by the authority in the name of Jesus Christ, no more frustration, I receive the anointing for ministerial success today.
13. I stand upon the Word of God and decree by the authority in the name of Jesus Christ, no more frustration, I receive the anointing for great achievements today.
14. I stand upon the Word of God and decree by the authority in the name of Jesus Christ, no more frustration, I receive the anointing for divine healing today.
15. By the power and authority in the blood of Jesus Christ, I withdraw the control of my life from the hands and

domination of the spirit of frustration, in the name of Jesus Christ.

16. By the power and authority in the blood of Jesus Christ, I withdraw the control of my finances from the hands and domination of the spirit of frustration, in the name of Jesus Christ.

17. By the power and authority in the blood of Jesus Christ, I withdraw the control of my family from the hands and domination of the spirit of frustration, in the name of Jesus Christ.

18. By the power and authority in the blood of Jesus Christ, I withdraw the control of my marriage from the hands and domination of the spirit of frustration, in the name of Jesus Christ.

19. By the power and authority in the blood of Jesus Christ, I withdraw the control of the life of my spouse from the hands and domination of the spirit of frustration, in the name of Jesus Christ.

20. By the power and authority in the blood of Jesus Christ, I withdraw the control of the life of my children from the hands and domination of the spirit of frustration, in the name of Jesus Christ.

21. By the power and authority in the blood of Jesus Christ, I withdraw the control of my ministry from the hands and domination of the spirit of frustration, in the name of Jesus Christ.

22. By the power and authority in the blood of Jesus Christ, I withdraw the control of my business from the hands and domination of the spirit of frustration, in the name of Jesus Christ.

23. By the power and authority in the blood of Jesus Christ, I withdraw the control of my destiny from the hands and

domination of the spirit of frustration, in the name of Jesus Christ.
24. By the power and authority in the blood of Jesus Christ, I withdraw the control of my future from the hands and domination of the spirit of frustration, in the name of Jesus Christ.
25. By the power and authority in the blood of Jesus Christ, I withdraw the control of my goals from the hands and domination of the spirit of frustration, in the name of Jesus Christ.
26. By the power and authority in the blood of Jesus Christ, I withdraw the control of my dreams from the hands and domination of the spirit of frustration, in the name of Jesus Christ.
27. By the power and authority in the blood of Jesus Christ, I withdraw the control of my prayer life from the hands and domination of the spirit of frustration, in the name of Jesus Christ.
28. O God my Father, arise and deliver me today from the bondage of frustration, in the name of Jesus Christ.
29. O God my Father, arise and deliver my family today from the bondage of frustration, in the name of Jesus Christ.
30. O God my Father, arise and deliver my marriage today from the bondage of frustration, in the name of Jesus Christ.
31. O God my Father, arise and deliver my spouse today from the bondage of frustration, in the name of Jesus Christ.
32. O God my Father, arise and deliver my children today from the bondage of frustration, in the name of Jesus Christ.

33. O God my Father, arise and deliver my finances today from the bondage of frustration, in the name of Jesus Christ.
34. Glory to God! The curse of frustration is finally and permanently broken over my life, I am free in the name of Jesus Christ.
35. Glory to God! The curse of frustration is finally and permanently broken over my family, we are free in the name of Jesus Christ.
36. Glory to God! The curse of frustration is finally and permanently broken over my marriage, we are free in the name of Jesus Christ.
37. Glory to God! The curse of frustration is finally and permanently broken over my ministry, I am free in the name of Jesus Christ.
38. Glory to God! The curse of frustration is finally and permanently broken over every area of my life, I am free in the name of Jesus Christ.

DELIVERANCE FROM ANCESTRAL CURSES OF MARITAL DELAY

(7 DAYS FASTING & INTENSIVE PRAYER)

KEY BIBLE PASSAGE

"And the LORD God said, It is not good that the man should be alone; I will make him an help meet for him. And out of the ground the LORD God formed every beast of the field, and every fowl of the air; and brought them unto Adam to see what he would call them: and whatsoever Adam called every living creature, that was the name thereof. And Adam gave names to all cattle, and to the fowl of the air, and to every beast of the field; but for Adam there was not found an help meet for him.

And the LORD God caused a deep sleep to fall upon Adam, and he slept: and he took one of his ribs, and closed up the flesh instead thereof; And the rib, which the LORD God had taken from man, made he a woman, and brought her unto the man.

And Adam said, This is now bone of my bones, and flesh of my flesh: she shall be called Woman, because she was taken out of Man. Therefore shall a man leave his father and his mother, and shall cleave unto his wife: and they shall be one flesh. And they were both naked, the man and his wife, and were not ashamed."
– Genesis 2:18-25

DAY ONE

GENERATIONAL REPENTANCE

Passages To Read Before You Pray:
Exodus 20:1-5, Jeremiah 31:27-34, Daniel 9:1-19, Psalms 89

I stand on the word of God to claim my right as a child of the Kingdom, I cover myself in the blood of Jesus Christ, I cover my household and everything concerning me in the blood of Jesus Christ. I hereby charge this atmosphere by the blood of Jesus Christ and by the fire of the Holy Ghost. I command fresh fire of God to rest upon me now as in the day of Pentecost, let fresh anointing and new oil be released upon me now as I pray. I receive power and authority over the power and the kingdom of darkness, to root out and to pull down, to destroy and to throw down, to build and to plant; whatever I decree in this prayer shall be established; whatever I bind today shall be bound in heaven and whatever I loose today shall be loosed in heaven as it is written in the word of God. Let fresh fire of God be released on my prayer altar and my prayer life now, prince of Persia cannot hinder my prayer, territorial spirit of my neighborhood cannot hinder my prayer, household wickedness cannot hinder my prayer.

I can see my prayer attracting divine intervention. This is the day that the Lord has made, I will rejoice and be glad in it. This is the day that the Lord has chosen to set me free from any form of

bondage and break any form of curses upon my life; this is the day that I will receive a total and complete deliverance in every area of my life, today shall mark the beginning of a new thing in my life.

I am a child of God, born of the Spirit, redeemed by the blood of the Lamb. It is written concerning me that power and authority is given unto me over all devils and to cure diseases, I hereby take authority over any form of curses upon my life, be it ancestral, be it generational, be it demon-inflicted or self-inflicted; I command all curses upon my life to break now by the authority in the name of Jesus Christ. The Bible says, where the word of a king is, there is power; today I speak as a king with the authority and power of the King of kings, and I command every other power to bow in the name of Jesus Christ. I render any power behind any curse upon my life useless and ineffective; I overcome any form of distraction, spiritual laziness and slumber, before the end of this prayer session my testimonies shall manifest without delay by the power in the name of Jesus Christ. Amen!

PRAYER POINTS

1. God my Father, thank you for being my God, my Father and my friend.
2. God my Father, thank you for the privilege to know you and the power of the resurrection of Jesus Christ.
3. God my Father, thank you for always being there for me and with me.
4. God my Father, thank you for the great and mighty things that you are doing in my life.

5. God my Father, thank you for your provision and protection over me and my household.
6. God my Father, thank you for always answering my prayers.
7. God my Father, I confess and repent of all sins in my life or my ancestors' lives that have resulted in a curse upon my life or bloodline; forgive me Lord on the basis of your mercy and cleanse me by the blood of Jesus Christ.
8. God my Father, I confess today and repent of all sins of disobedience in my life or my ancestor's lives that have resulted in a curse upon my life or bloodline; forgive me Lord on the basis of your mercy and cleanse me by the blood of Jesus Christ.
9. God my Father, I confess today and repent of all sins of rebellion in my life or my ancestor's lives that have resulted in a curse upon my life or bloodline; forgive me Lord on the basis of your mercy and cleanse me by the blood of Jesus Christ.
10. God my Father, I confess today and repent of all sins of perversion in my life or my ancestor's lives that have resulted in a curse upon my life or bloodline; forgive me Lord on the basis of your mercy and cleanse me by the blood of Jesus Christ.
11. God my Father, I confess today and repent of all sins of witchcraft in my life or my ancestor's lives that have resulted in a curse upon my life or bloodline; forgive me Lord on the basis of your mercy and cleanse me by the blood of Jesus Christ.
12. God my Father, I confess today and repent of all sins of idolatry in my life or my ancestor's lives that have resulted in a curse upon my life or bloodline; forgive

me Lord on the basis of your mercy and cleanse me by the blood of Jesus Christ.

13. God my Father, I confess today and repent of all sins of lust in my life or my ancestor's lives that have resulted in a curse upon my life or bloodline; forgive me Lord on the basis of your mercy and cleanse me by the blood of Jesus Christ.

14. God my Father, I confess today and repent of all sins of adultery in my life or my ancestor's lives that have resulted in a curse upon my life or bloodline; forgive me Lord on the basis of your mercy and cleanse me by the blood of Jesus Christ.

15. God my Father, I confess today and repent of all sins of fornication in my life or my ancestor's lives that have resulted in a curse upon my life or bloodline; forgive me Lord on the basis of your mercy and cleanse me by the blood of Jesus Christ.

16. God my Father, I confess today and repent of all sins of mistreatment of others in my life or my ancestor's lives that have resulted in a curse upon my life or bloodline; forgive me Lord on the basis of your mercy and cleanse me by the blood of Jesus Christ.

17. God my Father, I confess today and repent of all sins of murder or abortion in my life or my ancestor's lives that have resulted in a curse upon my life or bloodline; forgive me Lord on the basis of your mercy and cleanse me by the blood of Jesus Christ.

18. God my Father, I confess today and repent of all sins of cheating in my life or my ancestor's lives that have resulted in a curse upon my life or bloodline; forgive me Lord on the basis of your mercy and cleanse me by the blood of Jesus Christ.

19. God my Father, I confess today and repent of all sins of lying in my life or my ancestor's lives that have resulted in a curse upon my life or bloodline; forgive me Lord on the basis of your mercy and cleanse me by the blood of Jesus Christ.
20. God my Father, I confess today and repent of all sins of sorcery in my life or my ancestor's lives that have resulted in a curse upon my life or bloodline; forgive me Lord on the basis of your mercy and cleanse me by the blood of Jesus Christ.
21. God my Father, I confess today and repent of all sins of divination in my life or my ancestor's lives that have resulted in a curse upon my life or bloodline; forgive me Lord on the basis of your mercy and cleanse me by the blood of Jesus Christ.
22. God my Father, I confess today and repent of all sins of occult involvement in my life or my ancestor's lives that have resulted in a curse upon my life or bloodline; forgive me Lord on the basis of your mercy and cleanse me by the blood of Jesus Christ.
23. I disassociate myself from all evil done by my ancestors by the power in the blood of Jesus Christ.
24. I disassociate myself from all evil attitudes done by my ancestors against the will and purpose of God, in the name of Jesus Christ.
25. With all my heart I disagree with all sins committed by my ancestors, Father Lord have mercy and cleanse me by the blood of Jesus Christ.
26. Today with all my heart I declare that I refuse to be like my parents, in the name of Jesus Christ.
27. Today with all my heart I declare that I refuse to be like any of my ancestors, in the name of Jesus Christ.

28. I refuse to suffer the same problems as my parents, I reject it; my heart, soul, spirit and body reject it in the name of Jesus Christ.
29. I refuse to suffer the same problems as any of my ancestors, I reject it; my heart, soul, spirit and body reject it in the name of Jesus Christ.
30. In the name of Jesus Christ, I refuse to go through what my parents went through, my case is different, I am a child of God and covered by the blood of Jesus Christ.
31. By the power and authority in the blood of Jesus Christ, I severe myself from my bloodline, in the name of Jesus Christ.
32. By the power and authority in the blood of Jesus Christ, I severe myself from the connection to any of my ancestors, in the name of Jesus Christ.
33. By the power and authority in the blood of Jesus Christ, I severe myself from spiritual connection to any of my ancestors, in the name of Jesus Christ.
34. By the power and authority in the blood of Jesus Christ, I severe myself from physical connection to any of my ancestors, in the name of Jesus Christ.
35. By the power and authority in the blood of Jesus Christ, I severe myself from emotional connection to any of my ancestors, in the name of Jesus Christ.
36. By the power and authority in the blood of Jesus Christ, I severe myself from mental connection to any of my ancestors, in the name of Jesus Christ.
37. By the power and authority in the blood of Jesus Christ, I severe myself from the connection to the idol of my father's house, in the name of Jesus Christ.

38. By the power and authority in the blood of Jesus Christ, I sever myself from the connection to the idol of my mother's house, in the name of Jesus Christ.
39. By the power and authority in the blood of Jesus Christ, I destroy every spiritual DNA that links me to my ancestors by the fire of God, in the name of Jesus Christ.
40. By the power and authority in the blood of Jesus Christ, I destroy every spiritual DNA that links my children to my ancestors by the fire of God, in the name of Jesus Christ.

DAY TWO

BREAKING ANCESTRAL CURSES OF MARITAL DELAY

Passages To Read Before You Pray:
Genesis 2:18-25, Psalms 30, 35, Galatians 3:13, Isaiah 10:27

I stand on the word of God to claim my right as a child of the Kingdom, I cover myself in the blood of Jesus Christ, I cover my household and everything concerning me in the blood of Jesus Christ. I hereby charge this atmosphere by the blood of Jesus Christ and by the fire of the Holy Ghost. I command fresh fire of God to rest upon me now as in the day of Pentecost, let fresh anointing and new oil be released upon me now as I pray. I receive power and authority over the power and the kingdom of darkness, to root out and to pull down, to destroy and to throw down, to build and to plant; whatever I decree in this prayer shall be established; whatever I bind today shall be bound in heaven and whatever I loose today shall be loosed in heaven as it is written in the word of God. Let fresh fire of God be released on my prayer altar and my prayer life now, prince of Persia cannot hinder my prayer, territorial spirit of my neighborhood cannot hinder my prayer, household wickedness cannot hinder my prayer.

I can see my prayer attracting divine intervention. This is the day that the Lord has made, I will rejoice and be glad in it. This is the day that the Lord has chosen to set me free from any form of

bondage and break any form of curses upon my life; this is the day that I will receive a total and complete deliverance in every area of my life, today shall mark the beginning of a new thing in my life.

I am a child of God, born of the Spirit, redeemed by the blood of the Lamb. It is written concerning me that power and authority is given unto me over all devils and to cure diseases, I hereby take authority over any form of curses upon my life, be it ancestral, be it generational, be it demon-inflicted or self-inflicted; I command all curses upon my life to break now by the authority in the name of Jesus Christ. The Bible says, where the word of a king is, there is power; today I speak as a king with the authority and power of the King of kings, and I command every other power to bow in the name of Jesus Christ. I render any power behind any curse upon my life useless and ineffective; I overcome any form of distraction, spiritual laziness and slumber, before the end of this prayer session my testimonies shall manifest without delay by the power in the name of Jesus Christ. Amen!

PRAYER POINTS

1. God my Father, thank you for being my God, my Father and my friend.
2. God my Father, thank you for the privilege to know you and the power of the resurrection of Jesus Christ.
3. God my Father, thank you for always being there for me and with me.
4. God my Father, thank you for the great and mighty things that you are doing in my life.

5. God my Father, thank you for your provision and protection over me and my household.
6. God my Father, thank you for always answering my prayers.
7. I confess my sins before you today and I ask you to forgive me on the basis of your mercy, in the name of Jesus Christ.
8. Wash me clean today O Lord by the blood of Jesus Christ.
9. I cover myself and my household with the blood of Jesus Christ.
10. My prayers today will not go in vain; my prayers will produce the desired results in the name of Jesus Christ.
11. By the power in the blood of Jesus Christ, I break every curse of marriage problem in my bloodline from my life to my past generations all the way to Adam the first man, in the name of Jesus Christ.
12. I take authority and break every of curse of marital delay flowing in my bloodline by the power in the name of Jesus Christ.
13. I take authority and break the curse of marital delay over my life by the power in the name of Jesus Christ.
14. I take authority and break the curse of marital delay that has been affecting every woman in my lineage, enough is enough, loose your hold over my life now, in the name of Jesus Christ.
15. I take authority and break the curse of marital delay causing women in my family to stay single, enough is enough, my case is different, loose your hold over my life now, in the name of Jesus Christ.
16. I take authority and break the curse of marital delay causing women in my family to die single, enough is

enough, my case is different, loose your hold over my life now, in the name of Jesus Christ.
17. I take authority and break the curse of marital delay causing women in my family to live a miserable life, enough is enough, my case is different, loose your hold over my life now, in the name of Jesus Christ.
18. Curses of marital delay causing women to become invisible to men, you have done enough in my life, I command you to break now by the power in the name of Jesus Christ.
19. Curses of marital delay causing women to become unattractive to men, you have done enough in my life, I command you to break now by the power in the name of Jesus Christ.
20. Curses of marital delay causing women to become undesirable to men, you have done enough in my life, I command you to break now by the power and authority in the name of Jesus Christ.
21. Curses of marital delay causing women to live in frustration, you have no power over my life, I command you to break now by the power and authority in the name of Jesus Christ.
22. It is time for me to get married; I remove every veil of marital delay and set it on fire in the name of Jesus Christ.
23. It is time for me to get married; I remove every satanic covering upon my life today by the power in the name of Jesus Christ.
24. It is time for me to get married; Father Lord, let the bone of my bones locate me now, in the name of Jesus Christ.
25. It is time for me to get married; Father Lord, let the flesh of my flesh locate me now, in the name of Jesus Christ.

26. It is time for me to get married; let the man of my dream locate me now, in the name of Jesus Christ.
27. It is time for me to get married; let the man you have prepared and ordained for me locate me now, in the name of Jesus Christ.
28. I refuse to remain single, every curse of marital delay upon my life I command you to break now by the fire of God, in the name of Jesus Christ.
29. It does not matter how long this curse has been upon my life, I command it to break now by the power in the name of Jesus Christ.
30. It does not matter how long this curse has been upon my life, I command it to be removed now by the power in the name of Jesus Christ.
31. It does not matter how long this curse has been upon my life, I break myself loose today from the curse of marital delay in the name of Jesus Christ.
32. I release myself today from every covenant of lateness in marriage by the power and authority in the name of Jesus Christ.
33. By the power and authority in the blood of Jesus Christ, I cancel every covenant of lateness in marriage, in the name of Jesus Christ.
34. Every covenant of lateness in marriage that has been in my bloodline since the beginning of time, I release the fire of God to go back to the foundation of my lineage and destroy every unprofitable covenant of lateness in marriage by the power in the name of Jesus Christ.
35. Every covenant of lateness in marriage that has been affecting women in my bloodline since the beginning of time, I release the fire of God to go back to my foundation and destroy every unprofitable covenant of

lateness in marriage by the power in the name of Jesus Christ.

36. Every covenant of lateness in marriage that has been holding women in my bloodline back since the beginning of time, I release the fire of God to go back to my foundation and destroy every unprofitable covenant of lateness in marriage by the power in the name of Jesus Christ.

37. Every covenant of lateness in marriage that has been forcing women in my bloodline to live alone since the beginning of time, I release the fire of God to go back to my foundation and destroy every unprofitable covenant of lateness in marriage by the power in the name of Jesus Christ.

38. Every covenant of lateness in marriage that has been forcing women in my bloodline to die alone since the beginning of time, I release the fire of God to go back to my foundation and destroy every unprofitable covenant of lateness in marriage by the power in the name of Jesus Christ.

39. Every covenant of lateness in marriage that has been forcing women in my bloodline to marry late since the beginning of time, I release the fire of God to go back to my foundation and destroy every unprofitable covenant of lateness in marriage by the power in the name of Jesus Christ.

40. I renounce and break all evil curses upon my life causing me to remain single, in the name of Jesus Christ.

DAY THREE

O LORD, I AM TIRED OF WAITING

Passages To Read Before You Pray:
Job 22:28, Psalms 38, 66, 70, 86, Proverbs 13:12

I stand on the word of God to claim my right as a child of the Kingdom, I cover myself in the blood of Jesus Christ, I cover my household and everything concerning me in the blood of Jesus Christ. I hereby charge this atmosphere by the blood of Jesus Christ and by the fire of the Holy Ghost. I command fresh fire of God to rest upon me now as in the day of Pentecost, let fresh anointing and new oil be released upon me now as I pray. I receive power and authority over the power and the kingdom of darkness, to root out and to pull down, to destroy and to throw down, to build and to plant; whatever I decree in this prayer shall be established; whatever I bind today shall be bound in heaven and whatever I loose today shall be loosed in heaven as it is written in the word of God. Let fresh fire of God be released on my prayer altar and my prayer life now, prince of Persia cannot hinder my prayer, territorial spirit of my neighborhood cannot hinder my prayer, household wickedness cannot hinder my prayer.

I can see my prayer attracting divine intervention. This is the day that the Lord has made, I will rejoice and be glad in it. This is the day that the Lord has chosen to set me free from any form of

bondage and break any form of curses upon my life; this is the day that I will receive a total and complete deliverance in every area of my life, today shall mark the beginning of a new thing in my life.

I am a child of God, born of the Spirit, redeemed by the blood of the Lamb. It is written concerning me that power and authority is given unto me over all devils and to cure diseases, I hereby take authority over any form of curses upon my life, be it ancestral, be it generational, be it demon-inflicted or self-inflicted; I command all curses upon my life to break now by the authority in the name of Jesus Christ. The Bible says, where the word of a king is, there is power; today I speak as a king with the authority and power of the King of kings, and I command every other power to bow in the name of Jesus Christ. I render any power behind any curse upon my life useless and ineffective; I overcome any form of distraction, spiritual laziness and slumber, before the end of this prayer session my testimonies shall manifest without delay by the power in the name of Jesus Christ. Amen!

PRAYER POINTS

1. O God my Father, thank you for being my God, my Father and my friend.
2. O God my Father, thank you for the privilege to know you and the power of the resurrection of Jesus Christ.
3. O God my Father, thank you for always being there for me and with me.
4. O God my Father, thank you for the great and mighty things that you are doing in my life.

5. O God my Father, thank you for your provision and protection over me and my household.
6. O God my Father, thank you for always answering my prayers.
7. I confess my sins before you today and I ask you to forgive me on the basis of your mercy, in the name of Jesus Christ.
8. Wash me clean today O Lord by the blood of Jesus Christ.
9. I cover myself and my household with the blood of Jesus Christ.
10. My prayers today will not go in vain; my prayers will produce the desired results in the name of Jesus Christ.
11. O God my Father, I am tired of waiting, let my husband find me now in the name of Jesus Christ.
12. O God my Father, I am tired of waiting, let the man of your own heart locate me now, in the name of Jesus Christ.
13. I take authority over the strongman working against my marriage, loose your hold over my life now, in the name of Jesus Christ.
14. I arrest the strongman working against my marriage; I bind and cast you out of my life now by the power and authority in the name of Jesus Christ.
15. I arrest the strongman working against my future; I bind and cast you out of my life now by the power and authority in the name of Jesus Christ.
16. I stand on the word of God and break every marital curse placed on my life by the enemy, in the name of Jesus Christ.

17. I stand on the word of God and break every marital curse placed on my life by the household wickedness, in the name of Jesus Christ.
18. I stand on the word of God and break every marital curse placed on my life by the power of witchcraft, in the name of Jesus Christ.
19. I stand on the word of God and break every marital curse placed on my life by Jezebel spirit, in the name of Jesus Christ.
20. I stand on the word of God and break every marital curse that I ignorantly placed on myself, in the name of Jesus Christ.
21. I stand on the word of God and break every marital curse placed on my life by my parents, in the name of Jesus Christ.
22. I stand on the word of God and break every marital curse placed on my life by my ex-boyfriends, in the name of Jesus Christ.
23. I stand on the word of God and break every marital curse placed on my life by my ex-fiancé, in the name of Jesus Christ.
24. Any power anywhere that says I will not get married, you are a liar, it is my turn to get married and you will be put to shame, in the name of Jesus Christ.
25. By the power and authority in the blood of Jesus Christ, I stand against every spirit of discouragement, fear, worry and frustration; I bind and cast them out of my life now, in the name of Jesus Christ
26. Every demon connected to the curse of marital delay in my life, I command you to release me now in the name of Jesus Christ.

27. Every power connected to the curse of marital delay in my life, I command you to release me now in the name of Jesus Christ.
28. Principalities connected to the curse of marital delay in my life, I command you to release me now in the name of Jesus Christ.
29. Spiritual wickedness connected to the curse of marital delay in my life, I command you to release me now in the name of Jesus Christ.
30. Spiritual Pharaoh of my father's house connected to the curse of marital delay in my life, I command you to release me now in the name of Jesus Christ.
31. Spiritual Goliath of my father's house connected to the curse of marital delay in my life, I command you to release me now in the name of Jesus Christ.
32. Anything in my life that is anti-marriage in nature, I command you to disappear by the fire of God, in the name of Jesus Christ.
33. Anything in my home that is anti-marriage in nature, I command you to disappear by the fire of God, in the name of Jesus Christ.
34. Anything in my character that is anti-marriage in nature, I command you to disappear by the fire of God, in the name of Jesus Christ.
35. Anything around me that is anti-marriage in nature, I command you to disappear by the fire of God, in the name of Jesus Christ.
36. Anything in my work that is anti-marriage in nature, I command you to disappear by the fire of God, in the name of Jesus Christ.

37. Anything in my speech that is anti-marriage in nature, I command you to disappear by the fire of God, in the name of Jesus Christ.
38. Anything in my appearance that is anti-marriage in nature, I command you to disappear by the fire of God, in the name of Jesus Christ.
39. Anything in my countenance that is anti-marriage in nature, I command you to disappear by the fire of God, in the name of Jesus Christ.
40. Anything in my body that is anti-marriage in nature, I command you to disappear by the fire of God, in the name of Jesus Christ.

DAY FOUR

BREAKING SOUL-TIES

Passages To Read Before You Pray:
Revelation 12:11, Proverbs 18:22, Psalms 35, 70, 140, 83

I stand on the word of God to claim my right as a child of the Kingdom, I cover myself in the blood of Jesus Christ, I cover my household and everything concerning me in the blood of Jesus Christ. I hereby charge this atmosphere by the blood of Jesus Christ and by the fire of the Holy Ghost. I command fresh fire of God to rest upon me now as in the day of Pentecost, let fresh anointing and new oil be released upon me now as I pray. I receive power and authority over the power and the kingdom of darkness, to root out and to pull down, to destroy and to throw down, to build and to plant; whatever I decree in this prayer shall be established; whatever I bind today shall be bound in heaven and whatever I loose today shall be loosed in heaven as it is written in the word of God. Let fresh fire of God be released on my prayer altar and my prayer life now, prince of Persia cannot hinder my prayer, territorial spirit of my neighborhood cannot hinder my prayer, household wickedness cannot hinder my prayer.

I can see my prayer attracting divine intervention. This is the day that the Lord has made, I will rejoice and be glad in it. This is the day that the Lord has chosen to set me free from any form of

bondage and break any form of curses upon my life; this is the day that I will receive a total and complete deliverance in every area of my life, today shall mark the beginning of a new thing in my life.

I am a child of God, born of the Spirit, redeemed by the blood of the Lamb. It is written concerning me that power and authority is given unto me over all devils and to cure diseases, I hereby take authority over any form of curses upon my life, be it ancestral, be it generational, be it demon-inflicted or self-inflicted; I command all curses upon my life to break now by the authority in the name of Jesus Christ. The Bible says, where the word of a king is, there is power; today I speak as a king with the authority and power of the King of kings, and I command every other power to bow in the name of Jesus Christ. I render any power behind any curse upon my life useless and ineffective; I overcome any form of distraction, spiritual laziness and slumber, before the end of this prayer session my testimonies shall manifest without delay by the power in the name of Jesus Christ. Amen!

PRAYER POINTS

1. O God my Father, thank you for being my God, my Father and my friend.
2. O God my Father, thank you for the privilege to know you and the power of the resurrection of Jesus Christ.
3. O God my Father, thank you for always being there for me and with me.
4. O God my Father, thank you for the great and mighty things that you are doing in my life.

5. O God my Father, thank you for your provision and protection over me and my household.
6. O God my Father, thank you for always answering my prayers.
7. I confess my sins before you today and I ask you to forgive me on the basis of your mercy, in the name of Jesus Christ.
8. Wash me clean today O Lord by the blood of Jesus Christ.
9. I cover myself and my household with the blood of Jesus Christ.
10. My prayers today will not go in vain; my prayers will produce the desired results in the name of Jesus Christ.
11. O God my Father, reveal unto now, the bone of my bones and flesh of my flesh, in the name of Jesus Christ.
12. I refuse to follow evil pattern of marital delay programmed by any of my ancestors, in the name of Jesus Christ.
13. I revoke any spiritual marriage or child birth contrary to the will of God, in the name of Jesus Christ.
14. I annul every spiritual marriage causing marital delay in my life by the power and authority in the name of Jesus Christ.
15. I release the fire of God into my foundation to destroy every evil carryover from my ancestor affecting my marriage, in the name of Jesus Christ.
16. I release the fire of God into my foundation to destroy every evil carryover from my ancestor affecting my destiny, in the name of Jesus Christ.
17. I release the fire of God into my foundation to destroy every evil carryover from my ancestor affecting my life, in the name of Jesus Christ.

18. I dissolve every spiritual engagement conducted on my behalf by the fire of God, in the name of Jesus Christ.
19. I reject and renounce every spiritual dowry paid or received on my behalf by the fire of God, in the name of Jesus Christ.
20. I annul every spiritual wedding conducted on my behalf; it shall not stand because it is not of God, in the name of Jesus Christ.
21. I speak destruction to the root of oppression and affliction in my marital journey, in the name of Jesus Christ.
22. I arrest every ancestral spirit husband fighting against my physical marriage, I command you to loose your hold over my life now, in the name of Jesus Christ.
23. I arrest every ancestral spirit husband causing marital delay in my life, I command you to loose your hold over my life now, in the name of Jesus Christ.
24. I arrest every ancestral spirit husband causing me to live a miserable life, I command you to loose your hold over my life now, in the name of Jesus Christ.
25. I arrest every ancestral spirit husband covering me with evil veil that men would not see me, I command you to loose your hold over my life now, in the name of Jesus Christ.
26. I arrest every ancestral spirit husband causing me look like another person in the sight of men, I command you to loose your hold over my life now, in the name of Jesus Christ.
27. I arrest every ancestral spirit husband that is jealous over me, I command you to loose your hold over my life now, in the name of Jesus Christ.

28. I arrest every ancestral spirit husband that refuses to let me get married in the physical, I command you to loose your hold over my life now, in the name of Jesus Christ.
29. By the power and authority in the blood of Jesus Christ, I break every curse of loneliness over my life in the name of Jesus Christ.
30. By the power and authority in the blood of Jesus Christ, I break every covenant of loneliness in my life, in the name of Jesus Christ.
31. You power of error in choosing marriage partner, loose your hold over my life now in the name of Jesus Christ.
32. Holy Spirit of God, open my eyes to recognize the man who will be husband, in the name of Jesus Christ.
33. By the power and authority in the blood of Jesus Christ, I arrest the strongman in charge of marital failure in my family, loose your hold over my life now, my case is different, in the name of Jesus Christ.
34. By the power and authority in the blood of Jesus Christ, I arrest the strongman in charge of marital delay in my family, loose your hold over my life now, my case is different, in the name of Jesus Christ.
35. By the power and authority in the blood of Jesus Christ, I break every yoke of failure attached to my marital destiny, in the name of Jesus Christ.
36. O God my Father, let every imagination of the enemy against my marital life be rendered useless, in the name of Jesus Christ.
37. I refuse to co-operate with any anti-marriage spell and curses in the name of Jesus Christ.
38. I refuse to co-operate with the plan of the enemy concerning my marriage, in the name of Jesus Christ.

39. I refuse to co-operate with the agenda of the household wickedness concerning my marriage, in the name of Jesus Christ.
40. My prayers today will bring a positive turn to my situation in the name of Jesus Christ.

DAY FIVE

PRAYER TO ERASE EVIL MARKS

Passages To Read Before You Pray:
Isaiah 34:16, Ecclesiastes 3:11, Psalms 55, 109, 128, Colossians 2:14-15, Philippians 2:9-11

I stand on the word of God to claim my right as a child of the Kingdom, I cover myself in the blood of Jesus Christ, I cover my household and everything concerning me in the blood of Jesus Christ. I hereby charge this atmosphere by the blood of Jesus Christ and by the fire of the Holy Ghost. I command fresh fire of God to rest upon me now as in the day of Pentecost, let fresh anointing and new oil be released upon me now as I pray. I receive power and authority over the power and the kingdom of darkness, to root out and to pull down, to destroy and to throw down, to build and to plant; whatever I decree in this prayer shall be established; whatever I bind today shall be bound in heaven and whatever I loose today shall be loosed in heaven as it is written in the word of God. Let fresh fire of God be released on my prayer altar and my prayer life now, prince of Persia cannot hinder my prayer, territorial spirit of my neighborhood cannot hinder my prayer, household wickedness cannot hinder my prayer.

I can see my prayer attracting divine intervention. This is the day that the Lord has made, I will rejoice and be glad in it. This is the

day that the Lord has chosen to set me free from any form of bondage and break any form of curses upon my life; this is the day that I will receive a total and complete deliverance in every area of my life, today shall mark the beginning of a new thing in my life.

I am a child of God, born of the Spirit, redeemed by the blood of the Lamb. It is written concerning me that power and authority is given unto me over all devils and to cure diseases, I hereby take authority over any form of curses upon my life, be it ancestral, be it generational, be it demon-inflicted or self-inflicted; I command all curses upon my life to break now by the authority in the name of Jesus Christ. The Bible says, where the word of a king is, there is power; today I speak as a king with the authority and power of the King of kings, and I command every other power to bow in the name of Jesus Christ. I render any power behind any curse upon my life useless and ineffective; I overcome any form of distraction, spiritual laziness and slumber, before the end of this prayer session my testimonies shall manifest without delay by the power in the name of Jesus Christ. Amen!

PRAYER POINTS

1. O God my Father, thank you for being my God, my Father and my friend.
2. O God my Father, thank you for the privilege to know you and the power of the resurrection of Jesus Christ.
3. O God my Father, thank you for always being there for me and with me.

4. O God my Father, thank you for the great and mighty things that you are doing in my life.
5. O God my Father, thank you for your provision and protection over me and my household.
6. O God my Father, thank you for always answering my prayers.
7. I confess my sins before you today and I ask you to forgive me on the basis of your mercy, in the name of Jesus Christ.
8. Wash me clean today O Lord by the blood of Jesus Christ.
9. I cover myself and my household with the blood of Jesus Christ.
10. My prayers today will not go in vain; my prayers will produce the desired results in the name of Jesus Christ.
11. Every curse placed upon my life when I was in the womb causing my marital delay, I command it to break now by the power and authority in the name of Jesus Christ.
12. Every curse placed upon my mother before or after I was born causing my marital delay, I command you to break now by the power and authority in the name of Jesus Christ.
13. Any evil done to me when I was born that is now causing my marital delay, I command you to break now by the power and authority in the name of Jesus Christ.
14. Every curse placed upon my life when I was a little girl now causing my marital delay, I command you to break now by the power and authority in the name of Jesus Christ.

15. Every curse placed upon me when I was a teenager now causing my marital delay, I command you to break now by the power and authority in the name of Jesus Christ.
16. Every curse placed upon me because I refused to go on a date with any man, causing marital delay in my life, I command you to break now by the power and authority in the name of Jesus Christ.
17. Every curse placed upon me because I broke any man's heart, causing marital delay in my life, I command you to break now by the power and authority in the name of Jesus Christ.
18. Every curse placed upon my life as a result of what I did, now causing marital delay in my life, I command you to break now by the power and authority in the name of Jesus Christ.
19. Any power anywhere working against my settling down in marriage, you will not escape the judgment of God, in the name of Jesus Christ.
20. Principalities working against my settling down in marriage, you will not escape the judgment of God, in the name of Jesus Christ.
21. Household wickedness working against my settling down in marriage, you will not escape the judgment of God, in the name of Jesus Christ.
22. Unfriendly friend working against my settling down in marriage, you will not escape the judgment of God, in the name of Jesus Christ.
23. Demons of my father's house working against my settling down in marriage, you will not escape the judgment of God, in the name of Jesus Christ.

24. O God my Father, let every force magnetizing wrong men to me be disgrace and become useless, in the name of Jesus Christ.
25. By the power and authority in the blood of Jesus Christ, I remove the hands of the enemy from my marital life, in the name of Jesus Christ.
26. By the power and authority in the blood of Jesus Christ, I remove the hands of the household wickedness from my marital life, in the name of Jesus Christ.
27. By the power and authority in the blood of Jesus Christ, I remove the hands of the devil from my marital life, in the name of Jesus Christ.
28. By the power and authority in the blood of Jesus Christ, I remove the hands of unfriendly friends from my marital life, in the name of Jesus Christ.
29. By the power and authority in the blood of Jesus Christ, I remove the hands of my jealous friends from my marital life, in the name of Jesus Christ.
30. By the power and authority in the blood of Jesus Christ, I remove the hands of evil counselors from my marital life, in the name of Jesus Christ.
31. By the power and authority in the blood of Jesus Christ, I remove every evil mark of the enemy from my marital life, in the name of Jesus Christ.
32. By the power and authority in the blood of Jesus Christ, I remove every evil mark of the household wickedness from my marital life, in the name of Jesus Christ.
33. By the power and authority in the blood of Jesus Christ, I remove every evil mark of the devil from my marital life, in the name of Jesus Christ.

34. By the power and authority in the blood of Jesus Christ, I remove every evil mark of unfriendly friends from my marital life, in the name of Jesus Christ.
35. By the power and authority in the blood of Jesus Christ, I remove every evil mark of jealous friends from my marital life, in the name of Jesus Christ.
36. By the power and authority in the blood of Jesus Christ, I remove every evil mark of evil counselors from my marital life, in the name of Jesus Christ.
37. O God my Father, let all evil anti-marriage marks upon my life be removed now by the power in the blood of Jesus Christ.
38. O God my Father, let all evil anti-marriage marks upon my body be removed now by the power in the blood of Jesus Christ.
39. O God my Father, restore me to the perfect way in which you created me if my life has been altered in the name of Jesus Christ.
40. O God my Father, let your fire destroy every satanic weapon fashioned against my marriage, in the name of Jesus Christ.

DAY SIX

BREAKING STRONGHOLD OF MARITAL DELAY

Passages To Read Before You Pray:
2 Corinthians 10:3-6, Exodus 14:13-14, Psalms 29, 42, 3, 9, 140

I stand on the word of God to claim my right as a child of the Kingdom, I cover myself in the blood of Jesus Christ, I cover my household and everything concerning me in the blood of Jesus Christ. I hereby charge this atmosphere by the blood of Jesus Christ and by the fire of the Holy Ghost. I command fresh fire of God to rest upon me now as in the day of Pentecost, let fresh anointing and new oil be released upon me now as I pray. I receive power and authority over the power and the kingdom of darkness, to root out and to pull down, to destroy and to throw down, to build and to plant; whatever I decree in this prayer shall be established; whatever I bind today shall be bound in heaven and whatever I loose today shall be loosed in heaven as it is written in the word of God. Let fresh fire of God be released on my prayer altar and my prayer life now, prince of Persia cannot hinder my prayer, territorial spirit of my neighborhood cannot hinder my prayer, household wickedness cannot hinder my prayer.

I can see my prayer attracting divine intervention. This is the day that the Lord has made, I will rejoice and be glad in it. This is the day that the Lord has chosen to set me free from any form of

bondage and break any form of curses upon my life; this is the day that I will receive a total and complete deliverance in every area of my life, today shall mark the beginning of a new thing in my life.

I am a child of God, born of the Spirit, redeemed by the blood of the Lamb. It is written concerning me that power and authority is given unto me over all devils and to cure diseases, I hereby take authority over any form of curses upon my life, be it ancestral, be it generational, be it demon-inflicted or self-inflicted; I command all curses upon my life to break now by the authority in the name of Jesus Christ. The Bible says, where the word of a king is, there is power; today I speak as a king with the authority and power of the King of kings, and I command every other power to bow in the name of Jesus Christ. I render any power behind any curse upon my life useless and ineffective; I overcome any form of distraction, spiritual laziness and slumber, before the end of this prayer session my testimonies shall manifest without delay by the power in the name of Jesus Christ. Amen!

PRAYER POINTS

1. O God my Father, thank you for being my God, my Father and my friend.
2. O God my Father, thank you for the privilege to know you and the power of the resurrection of Jesus Christ.
3. O God my Father, thank you for always being there for me and with me.
4. O God my Father, thank you for the great and mighty things that you are doing in my life.

5. O God my Father, thank you for your provision and protection over me and my household.
6. O God my Father, thank you for always answering my prayers.
7. I confess my sins before you today and I ask you to forgive me on the basis of your mercy, in the name of Jesus Christ.
8. Wash me clean today O Lord by the blood of Jesus Christ.
9. I cover myself and my household with the blood of Jesus Christ.
10. My prayers today will not go in vain; my prayers will produce the desired results in the name of Jesus Christ.
11. O God my Father, expose all the schemes and plans of the devil ever devised against me through any source at any time in the name of Jesus Christ.
12. I forsake any personal sin that has given the enemy legal ground over my marital situation, in the name of Jesus Christ.
13. By the power and authority in the blood of Jesus Christ, I reclaim all the ground that I have lost to the enemy concerning my marital situation, in the name of Jesus Christ.
14. I apply the power in the blood of Jesus Christ to my marital situation today, in the name of Jesus Christ.
15. I apply the power in the name of Jesus Christ to my marital situation today, enough is enough.
16. I apply the power in the word of God to my marital situation today, in the name of Jesus Christ.
17. I apply the blood of Jesus Christ to remove all consequences of evil that I have done in the past on the

basis of the mercy of God, it shall no longer affect me or my marital life in the name of Jesus Christ.
18. By the power and authority in the blood of Jesus Christ, I break the binding effect of anything evil ever put on me from any source causing marital delay, in the name of Jesus Christ.
19. I sever myself from any satanic linkage and any strange power causing my marital delay, in the name of Jesus Christ.
20. By the power and authority in the blood of Jesus Christ, I remove the right of the enemy to afflict my plan to get married, in the name of Jesus Christ.
21. By the power and authority in the blood of Jesus Christ, I break the bondage of inherited marital confusion over my life in the name of Jesus Christ.
22. By the power and authority in the name of Jesus Christ, I command angels of the living God to roll away any stone blocking my marital breakthrough.
23. Let God arise and let all the enemies of my marital breakthroughs be scattered, in the name of Jesus Christ.
24. O God my Father, let your fire melt away the stones hindering my marital breakthrough, in the name of Jesus Christ.
25. O God my Father, let your fire melt away the stones hindering my marital blessings, in the name of Jesus Christ.
26. Every chain of marital delay, I command you to break now by the power in the name of Jesus Christ.
27. By the power in the blood of Jesus Christ, I pull down every stronghold of satanic delay in my marital life, in the name of Jesus Christ.

28. By the power and authority in the blood of Jesus Christ, I command every mark of ancestral marital failure in my life to be erased completely, in the name of Jesus Christ.
29. By the power and authority in the blood of Jesus Christ, I command every mark of ancestral marital delay in my life to be erased completely, in the name of Jesus Christ.
30. By the power and authority in the blood of Jesus Christ, I command every mark of ancestral marital disappointment in my life to be erased completely, in the name of Jesus Christ.
31. By the power and authority in the blood of Jesus Christ, I command every mark of ancestral loneliness in my life to be erased completely, in the name of Jesus Christ.
32. By the power and authority in the blood of Jesus Christ, I command every evil wall between me and the man that God has choosing for me to come down now, in the name of Jesus Christ.
33. By the power and authority in the blood of Jesus Christ, I overthrow every evil plan against my marriage, I am getting married this year and the enemy cannot stop me because it is ordained by God, in the name of Jesus Christ.
34. O God my Father, I refuse to be alone, let my helpmate locate me now in the name of Jesus Christ.
35. It is written that he that finds a wife finds a good thing; let my godly husband find me now in the name of Jesus Christ.
36. O God my Father, bless me today with a husband that will honor and cherish me in the name of Jesus Christ.
37. O God my Father, bless me today with a husband that will love me as Christ loves the church in the name of Jesus Christ.

38. O God my Father, bless me today with a husband that will love me as his own body in the name of Jesus Christ.
39. O God my Father, bless me today with a husband that his life is filled with the fear of God, in the name of Jesus Christ.
40. O God my Father, bless me today with a husband who lives a spirit filled life in the name of Jesus Christ.

DAY SEVEN

I SHALL NOT MAKE MISTAKE

Passages To Read Before You Pray:
Exodus 13:21-22, Ecclesiastes 4:9-12, Psalms 37, 44, 70, 60

I stand on the word of God to claim my right as a child of the Kingdom, I cover myself in the blood of Jesus Christ, I cover my household and everything concerning me in the blood of Jesus Christ. I hereby charge this atmosphere by the blood of Jesus Christ and by the fire of the Holy Ghost. I command fresh fire of God to rest upon me now as in the day of Pentecost, let fresh anointing and new oil be released upon me now as I pray. I receive power and authority over the power and the kingdom of darkness, to root out and to pull down, to destroy and to throw down, to build and to plant; whatever I decree in this prayer shall be established; whatever I bind today shall be bound in heaven and whatever I loose today shall be loosed in heaven as it is written in the word of God. Let fresh fire of God be released on my prayer altar and my prayer life now, prince of Persia cannot hinder my prayer, territorial spirit of my neighborhood cannot hinder my prayer, household wickedness cannot hinder my prayer.

I can see my prayer attracting divine intervention. This is the day that the Lord has made, I will rejoice and be glad in it. This is the day that the Lord has chosen to set me free from any form of

bondage and break any form of curses upon my life; this is the day that I will receive a total and complete deliverance in every area of my life, today shall mark the beginning of a new thing in my life.

I am a child of God, born of the Spirit, redeemed by the blood of the Lamb. It is written concerning me that power and authority is given unto me over all devils and to cure diseases, I hereby take authority over any form of curses upon my life, be it ancestral, be it generational, be it demon-inflicted or self-inflicted; I command all curses upon my life to break now by the authority in the name of Jesus Christ. The Bible says, where the word of a king is, there is power; today I speak as a king with the authority and power of the King of kings, and I command every other power to bow in the name of Jesus Christ. I render any power behind any curse upon my life useless and ineffective; I overcome any form of distraction, spiritual laziness and slumber, before the end of this prayer session my testimonies shall manifest without delay by the power in the name of Jesus Christ. Amen!

PRAYER POINTS

1. O God my Father, thank you for being my God, my Father and my friend.
2. O God my Father, thank you for the privilege to know you and the power of the resurrection of Jesus Christ.
3. O God my Father, thank you for always being there for me and with me.
4. O God my Father, thank you for the great and mighty things that you are doing in my life.

5. O God my Father, thank you for your provision and protection over me and my household.
6. O God my Father, thank you for always answering my prayers.
7. I confess my sins before you today and I ask you to forgive me on the basis of your mercy, in the name of Jesus Christ.
8. Wash me clean today O Lord by the blood of Jesus Christ.
9. I cover myself and my household with the blood of Jesus Christ.
10. My prayers today will not go in vain; my prayers will produce the desired results in the name of Jesus Christ.
11. O God my Father, bless me today with a husband that is not abusive but supportive and helpful, in the name of Jesus Christ.
12. O God my Father, bless me today with a husband that will give me freedom to serve you, so that we can both serve you in the name of Jesus Christ.
13. O God my Father, bless me today with a husband that will not kill my dream but help me to fulfill my dreams in the name of Jesus Christ.
14. O God my Father, bless me today with a man after your own heart in the name of Jesus Christ.
15. O God my Father, I refuse to make a mistake in marriage, help me to make the right decision in the name of Jesus Christ.
16. O God my Father, I refuse to make a mistake in marriage, grant me divine wisdom to make a wise decision in the name of Jesus Christ.
17. I refuse to allow the lust of the flesh to push me into making wrong decision, in the name of Jesus Christ.

18. I refuse to allow the lust of the eyes to lure me to make wrong decision in the name of Jesus Christ.
19. I refuse to allow anyone around me to force me into making wrong decision in marriage, in the name of Jesus Christ.
20. I refuse to allow any situation to force me to make wrong decision in marriage, in the name of Jesus Christ.
21. You spirit of lateness in marriage, I command you to release me now, it is my time and I am ready to get married, in the name of Jesus Christ.
22. You spirit of delay, I command you to release me now, it is my time and I am ready to get married, in the name of Jesus Christ.
23. Misfortune in every area of my life, I command you to release me now, it is my time and I am ready to get married, in the name of Jesus Christ.
24. Today I command my godly husband to come forth and locate me, in the name of Jesus Christ.
25. Today O Lord, it is high time, let my godly husband seek and find me in the name of Jesus Christ.
26. O God my Father, let my godly husband relocate to locate me in the name of Jesus Christ.
27. O God my Father, let my godly husband see your good hands upon my life in the name of Jesus Christ.
28. O God my Father, let my godly husband see your glory and honor upon my life in the name of Jesus Christ.
29. Today O Lord, put an end to loneliness in my life in the name of Jesus Christ.
30. It is written that two are better than one; bless me today with a godly husband that we can walk together in the Lord in the name of Jesus Christ.

31. It is written that two are better than one, bless me today with a godly husband that will work together with me to build our future, in the name of Jesus Christ.
32. O God my Father, bless me with a home that is full of love and joy, in the name of Jesus Christ.
33. O God my Father, bless me with a godly man that will not only be my husband but also my best friend forever, in the name of Jesus Christ.
34. O God my Father, bless me with a godly man that will not only be my husband but also my confidant and counselor, in the name of Jesus Christ.
35. O God my Father, bless me with a godly man that will not only be my husband but someone reliable and dependable, in the name of Jesus Christ.
36. O God my Father, bless me with a godly man that will not only be my husband but someone with vision and hardworking, in the name of Jesus Christ.
37. Every prayer that I have prayed today will produce the desired results in the name of Jesus Christ.
38. Every prayer that I have prayed today will bring forth testimonies in the name of Jesus Christ.
39. Miracles will follow my prayers in the name of Jesus Christ.
40. As I pray today, heaven will respond to my petition in the name of Jesus Christ.

DELIVERANCE FROM ANCESTRAL CURSES OF TRAGEDY

(5 DAYS FASTING & INTENSIVE PRAYER)

KEY BIBLE PASSAGE

"And God shall wipe away all tears from their eyes; and there shall be no more death, neither sorrow, nor crying, neither shall there be any more pain: for the former things are passed away."
– Revelation 21:4

DAY ONE

GENERATIONAL REPENTANCE

Passages To Read Before You Pray:
Exodus 20:1-5, Jeremiah 31:27-34, Daniel 9:1-19, Psalms 89

I stand on the word of God to claim my right as a child of the Kingdom, I cover myself in the blood of Jesus Christ, I cover my household and everything concerning me in the blood of Jesus Christ. I hereby charge this atmosphere by the blood of Jesus Christ and by the fire of the Holy Ghost. I command fresh fire of God to rest upon me now as in the day of Pentecost, let fresh anointing and new oil be released upon me now as I pray. I receive power and authority over the power and the kingdom of darkness, to root out and to pull down, to destroy and to throw down, to build and to plant; whatever I decree in this prayer shall be established; whatever I bind today shall be bound in heaven and whatever I loose today shall be loosed in heaven as it is written in the word of God. Let fresh fire of God be released on my prayer altar and my prayer life now, prince of Persia cannot hinder my prayer, territorial spirit of my neighborhood cannot hinder my prayer, household wickedness cannot hinder my prayer.

I can see my prayer attracting divine intervention. This is the day that the Lord has made, I will rejoice and be glad in it. This is the day that the Lord has chosen to set me free from any form of

bondage and break any form of curses upon my life; this is the day that I will receive a total and complete deliverance in every area of my life, today shall mark the beginning of a new thing in my life.

I am a child of God, born of the Spirit, redeemed by the blood of the Lamb. It is written concerning me that power and authority is given unto me over all devils and to cure diseases, I hereby take authority over any form of curses upon my life, be it ancestral, be it generational, be it demon-inflicted or self-inflicted; I command all curses upon my life to break now by the authority in the name of Jesus Christ. The Bible says, where the word of a king is, there is power; today I speak as a king with the authority and power of the King of kings, and I command every other power to bow in the name of Jesus Christ. I render any power behind any curse upon my life useless and ineffective; I overcome any form of distraction, spiritual laziness and slumber, before the end of this prayer session my testimonies shall manifest without delay by the power in the name of Jesus Christ. Amen!

PRAYER POINTS

1. God my Father, thank you for being my God, my Father and my friend.
2. God my Father, thank you for the privilege to know you and the power of the resurrection of Jesus Christ.
3. God my Father, thank you for always being there for me and with me.
4. God my Father, thank you for the great and mighty things that you are doing in my life.

5. God my Father, thank you for your provision and protection over me and my household.
6. God my Father, thank you for always answering my prayers.
7. God my Father, I confess and repent of all sins in my life or my ancestors' lives that have resulted in a curse upon my life or bloodline; forgive me Lord on the basis of your mercy and cleanse me by the blood of Jesus Christ.
8. God my Father, I confess today and repent of all sins of disobedience in my life or my ancestor's lives that have resulted in a curse upon my life or bloodline; forgive me Lord on the basis of your mercy and cleanse me by the blood of Jesus Christ.
9. God my Father, I confess today and repent of all sins of rebellion in my life or my ancestor's lives that have resulted in a curse upon my life or bloodline; forgive me Lord on the basis of your mercy and cleanse me by the blood of Jesus Christ.
10. God my Father, I confess today and repent of all sins of perversion in my life or my ancestor's lives that have resulted in a curse upon my life or bloodline; forgive me Lord on the basis of your mercy and cleanse me by the blood of Jesus Christ.
11. God my Father, I confess today and repent of all sins of witchcraft in my life or my ancestor's lives that have resulted in a curse upon my life or bloodline; forgive me Lord on the basis of your mercy and cleanse me by the blood of Jesus Christ.
12. God my Father, I confess today and repent of all sins of idolatry in my life or my ancestor's lives that have resulted in a curse upon my life or bloodline; forgive me

Lord on the basis of your mercy and cleanse me by the blood of Jesus Christ.

13. God my Father, I confess today and repent of all sins of lust in my life or my ancestor's lives that have resulted in a curse upon my life or bloodline; forgive me Lord on the basis of your mercy and cleanse me by the blood of Jesus Christ.

14. God my Father, I confess today and repent of all sins of adultery in my life or my ancestor's lives that have resulted in a curse upon my life or bloodline; forgive me Lord on the basis of your mercy and cleanse me by the blood of Jesus Christ.

15. God my Father, I confess today and repent of all sins of fornication in my life or my ancestor's lives that have resulted in a curse upon my life or bloodline; forgive me Lord on the basis of your mercy and cleanse me by the blood of Jesus Christ.

16. God my Father, I confess today and repent of all sins of mistreatment of others in my life or my ancestor's lives that have resulted in a curse upon my life or bloodline; forgive me Lord on the basis of your mercy and cleanse me by the blood of Jesus Christ.

17. God my Father, I confess today and repent of all sins of murder or abortion in my life or my ancestor's lives that have resulted in a curse upon my life or bloodline; forgive me Lord on the basis of your mercy and cleanse me by the blood of Jesus Christ.

18. God my Father, I confess today and repent of all sins of cheating in my life or my ancestor's lives that have resulted in a curse upon my life or bloodline; forgive me Lord on the basis of your mercy and cleanse me by the blood of Jesus Christ.

19. God my Father, I confess today and repent of all sins of lying in my life or my ancestor's lives that have resulted in a curse upon my life or bloodline; forgive me Lord on the basis of your mercy and cleanse me by the blood of Jesus Christ.
20. God my Father, I confess today and repent of all sins of sorcery in my life or my ancestor's lives that have resulted in a curse upon my life or bloodline; forgive me Lord on the basis of your mercy and cleanse me by the blood of Jesus Christ.
21. God my Father, I confess today and repent of all sins of divination in my life or my ancestor's lives that have resulted in a curse upon my life or bloodline; forgive me Lord on the basis of your mercy and cleanse me by the blood of Jesus Christ.
22. God my Father, I confess today and repent of all sins of occult involvement in my life or my ancestor's lives that have resulted in a curse upon my life or bloodline; forgive me Lord on the basis of your mercy and cleanse me by the blood of Jesus Christ.
23. I disassociate myself from all evil done by my ancestors by the power in the blood of Jesus Christ.
24. I disassociate myself from all evil attitudes done by my ancestors against the will and purpose of God, in the name of Jesus Christ.
25. With all my heart I disagree with all sins committed by my ancestors, Father Lord have mercy and cleanse me by the blood of Jesus Christ.
26. Today with all my heart I declare that I refuse to be like my parents, in the name of Jesus Christ.
27. Today with all my heart I declare that I refuse to be like any of my ancestors, in the name of Jesus Christ.

28. I refuse to suffer the same problems as my parents, I reject it; my heart, soul, spirit and body reject it in the name of Jesus Christ.
29. I refuse to suffer the same problems as any of my ancestors, I reject it; my heart, soul, spirit and body reject it in the name of Jesus Christ.
30. In the name of Jesus Christ, I refuse to go through what my parents went through, my case is different, I am a child of God and covered by the blood of Jesus Christ.
31. By the power and authority in the blood of Jesus Christ, I sever myself from my bloodline, in the name of Jesus Christ.
32. By the power and authority in the blood of Jesus Christ, I sever myself from the connection to any of my ancestors, in the name of Jesus Christ.
33. By the power and authority in the blood of Jesus Christ, I sever myself from spiritual connection to any of my ancestors, in the name of Jesus Christ.
34. By the power and authority in the blood of Jesus Christ, I sever myself from physical connection to any of my ancestors, in the name of Jesus Christ.
35. By the power and authority in the blood of Jesus Christ, I sever myself from emotional connection to any of my ancestors, in the name of Jesus Christ.
36. By the power and authority in the blood of Jesus Christ, I sever myself from mental connection to any of my ancestors, in the name of Jesus Christ.
37. By the power and authority in the blood of Jesus Christ, I sever myself from the connection to the idol of my father's house, in the name of Jesus Christ.

38. By the power and authority in the blood of Jesus Christ, I severe myself from the connection to the idol of my mother's house, in the name of Jesus Christ.
39. By the power and authority in the blood of Jesus Christ, I destroy every spiritual DNA that links me to my ancestors by the fire of God, in the name of Jesus Christ.
40. By the power and authority in the blood of Jesus Christ, I destroy every spiritual DNA that links my children to my ancestors by the fire of God, in the name of Jesus Christ.

DAY TWO

PRAYER TO DESTROY ROOTS OF SORROW

Passages To Read Before You Pray:
Revelation 21:4, Nehemiah 8:10, Psalms 34, 100, 59, 69, 55

I stand on the word of God to claim my right as a child of the Kingdom, I cover myself in the blood of Jesus Christ, I cover my household and everything concerning me in the blood of Jesus Christ. I hereby charge this atmosphere by the blood of Jesus Christ and by the fire of the Holy Ghost. I command fresh fire of God to rest upon me now as in the day of Pentecost, let fresh anointing and new oil be released upon me now as I pray. I receive power and authority over the power and the kingdom of darkness, to root out and to pull down, to destroy and to throw down, to build and to plant; whatever I decree in this prayer shall be established; whatever I bind today shall be bound in heaven and whatever I loose today shall be loosed in heaven as it is written in the word of God. Let fresh fire of God be released on my prayer altar and my prayer life now, prince of Persia cannot hinder my prayer, territorial spirit of my neighborhood cannot hinder my prayer, household wickedness cannot hinder my prayer.

I can see my prayer attracting divine intervention. This is the day that the Lord has made, I will rejoice and be glad in it. This is the day that the Lord has chosen to set me free from any form of

bondage and break any form of curses upon my life; this is the day that I will receive a total and complete deliverance in every area of my life, today shall mark the beginning of a new thing in my life.

I am a child of God, born of the Spirit, redeemed by the blood of the Lamb. It is written concerning me that power and authority is given unto me over all devils and to cure diseases, I hereby take authority over any form of curses upon my life, be it ancestral, be it generational, be it demon-inflicted or self-inflicted; I command all curses upon my life to break now by the authority in the name of Jesus Christ. The Bible says, where the word of a king is, there is power; today I speak as a king with the authority and power of the King of kings, and I command every other power to bow in the name of Jesus Christ. I render any power behind any curse upon my life useless and ineffective; I overcome any form of distraction, spiritual laziness and slumber, before the end of this prayer session my testimonies shall manifest without delay by the power in the name of Jesus Christ. Amen!

PRAYER POINTS

1. God my Father, thank you for being my God, my Father and my friend.
2. God my Father, thank you for the privilege to know you and the power of the resurrection of Jesus Christ.
3. God my Father, thank you for always being there for me and with me.
4. God my Father, thank you for the great and mighty things that you are doing in my life.

5. God my Father, thank you for your provision and protection over me and my household.
6. God my Father, thank you for always answering my prayers.
7. I confess my sins before you today and I ask you to forgive me on the basis of your mercy, in the name of Jesus Christ.
8. Wash me clean today O Lord by the blood of Jesus Christ.
9. I cover myself and my household with the blood of Jesus Christ.
10. My prayers today will not go in vain; my prayers will produce the desired results in the name of Jesus Christ.
11. By the power in the blood of Jesus Christ, I break every curse of tragedy in my bloodline from my life to my past generations all the way to Adam the first man, in the name of Jesus Christ.
12. I take authority and break every curse of tragedy upon my life by the power in the name of Jesus Christ.
13. I take authority and break every curse of tragedy upon my spouse by the power in the name of Jesus Christ.
14. I take authority and break every curse of tragedy upon my children by the power in the name of Jesus Christ.
15. I take authority and break every curse of tragedy upon my children's children by the power in the name of Jesus Christ.
16. I take authority and break every curse of tragedy upon my future generations by the power in the name of Jesus Christ.
17. I cut off any connection which my life may have with the spirit of tragedy by the fire of God, in the name of Jesus Christ.

18. I cut off any connection which my life may have with the spirit of tragedy from father's lineage by the fire of God, in the name of Jesus Christ.
19. I cut off any connection which my life may have with the spirit of tragedy from mother's lineage by the fire of God, in the name of Jesus Christ.
20. By the power and authority in the blood of Jesus Christ, concerning my life I cancel every appointment with sorrow, in the name of Jesus Christ.
21. By the power and authority in the blood of Jesus Christ, concerning my family I cancel every appointment with sorrow, in the name of Jesus Christ.
22. By the power and authority in the blood of Jesus Christ, concerning my marriage I cancel every appointment with sorrow, in the name of Jesus Christ.
23. By the power and authority in the blood of Jesus Christ, concerning my spouse I cancel every appointment with sorrow, in the name of Jesus Christ.
24. By the power and authority in the blood of Jesus Christ, concerning my children I cancel every appointment with sorrow, in the name of Jesus Christ.
25. By the power and authority in the blood of Jesus Christ, concerning my parents I cancel every appointment with sorrow, in the name of Jesus Christ.
26. By the power and authority in the blood of Jesus Christ, concerning my siblings I cancel every appointment with sorrow, in the name of Jesus Christ.
27. By the power and authority in the blood of Jesus Christ, concerning my friends I cancel every appointment with sorrow, in the name of Jesus Christ.

28. By the power and authority in the blood of Jesus Christ, concerning all my loved ones I cancel every appointment with sorrow, in the name of Jesus Christ.
29. Every curse of tragedy causing my ancestors to live in sorrow, you have no power over me, my case is difference, in the name of Jesus Christ.
30. Every curse of tragedy causing my ancestors to live in sorrow, you have no power over my family, loose hold upon my family now, in the name of Jesus Christ.
31. Every curse of tragedy causing my ancestors to live in sorrow, you have no power over my spouse, I command you to break now by the power in the name of Jesus Christ.
32. Every curse of tragedy causing my ancestors to live in sorrow, you have no power over my children, I command you to break now by the power in the name of Jesus Christ.
33. Every curse of tragedy causing my ancestors to live in sorrow, you have no power over my future generations, I command you to break now by the power in the name of Jesus Christ.
34. Every curse of tragedy that has been working in my bloodline from generation to generation, your time is up, I command you to break now by the power in the name of Jesus Christ.
35. Every curse of tragedy that has been taking lives of young men from the hands of their parents from generation to generation, you have no power over my life, I command you to break now by the power in the name of Jesus Christ.

DAY THREE

DELIVERANCE FROM ANCESTRAL CURSE OF TRAGEDY

Passages To Read Before You Pray:
Obadiah 1:17, Isaiah 10:27, Jeremiah 15:11, Psalms 140, 91, 40, 70, 86

I stand on the word of God to claim my right as a child of the Kingdom, I cover myself in the blood of Jesus Christ, I cover my household and everything concerning me in the blood of Jesus Christ. I hereby charge this atmosphere by the blood of Jesus Christ and by the fire of the Holy Ghost. I command fresh fire of God to rest upon me now as in the day of Pentecost, let fresh anointing and new oil be released upon me now as I pray. I receive power and authority over the power and the kingdom of darkness, to root out and to pull down, to destroy and to throw down, to build and to plant; whatever I decree in this prayer shall be established; whatever I bind today shall be bound in heaven and whatever I loose today shall be loosed in heaven as it is written in the word of God. Let fresh fire of God be released on my prayer altar and my prayer life now, prince of Persia cannot hinder my prayer, territorial spirit of my neighborhood cannot hinder my prayer, household wickedness cannot hinder my prayer.

I can see my prayer attracting divine intervention. This is the day that the Lord has made, I will rejoice and be glad in it. This is the day that the Lord has chosen to set me free from any form of bondage and break any form of curses upon my life; this is the day that I will receive a total and complete deliverance in every area of my life, today shall mark the beginning of a new thing in my life.

I am a child of God, born of the Spirit, redeemed by the blood of the Lamb. It is written concerning me that power and authority is given unto me over all devils and to cure diseases, I hereby take authority over any form of curses upon my life, be it ancestral, be it generational, be it demon-inflicted or self-inflicted; I command all curses upon my life to break now by the authority in the name of Jesus Christ. The Bible says, where the word of a king is, there is power; today I speak as a king with the authority and power of the King of kings, and I command every other power to bow in the name of Jesus Christ. I render any power behind any curse upon my life useless and ineffective; I overcome any form of distraction, spiritual laziness and slumber, before the end of this prayer session my testimonies shall manifest without delay by the power in the name of Jesus Christ. Amen!

PRAYER POINTS

1. O God my Father, thank you for being my God, my Father and my friend.
2. O God my Father, thank you for the privilege to know you and the power of the resurrection of Jesus Christ.

3. O God my Father, thank you for always being there for me and with me.
4. O God my Father, thank you for the great and mighty things that you are doing in my life.
5. O God my Father, thank you for your provision and protection over me and my household.
6. O God my Father, thank you for always answering my prayers.
7. I confess my sins before you today and I ask you to forgive me on the basis of your mercy, in the name of Jesus Christ.
8. Wash me clean today O Lord by the blood of Jesus Christ.
9. I cover myself and my household with the blood of Jesus Christ.
10. My prayers today will not go in vain; my prayers will produce the desired results in the name of Jesus Christ.
11. Every curse of tragedy that has been taking lives of young men from the hands of their parents from generation to generation, you have no power over my sons, I command you to break now by the power in the name of Jesus Christ.
12. Every curse of tragedy that has been taking lives of young men from the hands of their parents from generation to generation, you have no power over my brothers, I command you to break now by the power in the name of Jesus Christ.
13. Every curse of tragedy that has been taking lives of young men from the hands of their parents from generation to generation, you have no power over any of my loved ones, I command you to break now by the power in the name of Jesus Christ.

14. Every curse of tragedy that has been taking lives of young women from the hands of their parents from generation to generation, you have no power over my life, I command you to break now by the power in the name of Jesus Christ.
15. Every curse of tragedy that has been taking lives of young women from the hands of their parents from generation to generation, you have no power of my daughters, I command you to break now by the power in the name of Jesus Christ.
16. Every curse of tragedy that has been taking lives of young women from the hands of their parents from generation to generation, you have no power over my sisters, I command you to break now by the power in the name of Jesus Christ.
17. Every curse of tragedy that has been taking lives of young women from the hands of their parents from generation to generation, you have no power over any of my loved ones, I command you to break now by the power in the name of Jesus Christ.
18. Every curse of tragedy that has been taking lives of wives from the hands of their husbands from generation to generation, you have no power over me, I command you to break now by the power in the name of Jesus Christ.
19. Every curse of tragedy that has been taking lives of wives from the hands of their husbands from generation to generation, you have no power over my daughters, I command you to break now by the power in the name of Jesus Christ.
20. You curse of tragedy that has been taking lives of wives from the hands of their husbands from generation to

generation, you have no power over my sisters, I command you to break now by the power in the name of Jesus Christ.
21. Every curse of tragedy that has been taking lives of wives from the hands of their husbands from generation to generation, you have no power over any of my loved ones, I command you to break now by the power in the name of Jesus Christ.
22. Every curse of tragedy that has been taking lives of wives from the hands of their husbands from generation to generation, you have no power over my mother, I command you to break now by the power in the name of Jesus Christ.
23. Every curse of tragedy that has been taking lives of wives from the hands of their husbands from generation to generation, you have no power over my aunts, I command you to break now by the power in the name of Jesus Christ.
24. Every curse of tragedy that has been taking lives of wives from the hands of their husbands from generation to generation, you have no power over nieces, I command you to break now by the power in the name of Jesus Christ.
25. Every curse of tragedy that has been taking lives of husbands from the hands of their wives from generation to generation, you have no power over me, I command you to break now by the power in the name of Jesus Christ.
26. Every curse of tragedy that has been taking lives of husbands from the hands of their wives from generation to generation, you have no power over my sons, I

command you to break now by the power in the name of Jesus Christ.
27. Every curse of tragedy that has been taking lives of husbands from the hands of their wives from generation to generation, you have no power over my brothers, I command you to break now by the power in the name of Jesus Christ.
28. Every curse of tragedy that has been taking lives of husbands from the hands of their wives from generation to generation, you have no power over my father, I command you to break now by the power in the name of Jesus Christ.
29. Every curse of tragedy that has been taking lives of husbands from the hands of their wives from generation to generation, you have no power over my uncles, I command you to break now by the power in the name of Jesus Christ.
30. Every curse of tragedy that has been taking lives of husbands from the hands of their wives from generation to generation, you have no power over my nephews, I command you to break now by the power in the name of Jesus Christ.
31. Every curse of tragedy that has been taking lives of husbands from the hands of their wives from generation to generation, you have no power over any of my loved ones, I command you to break now by the power in the name of Jesus Christ.
32. Every curse of tragedy that has been taking people's lives before the day of their joy from generation to generation, your assignment is over, I command you to break now over my life in the name of Jesus Christ.

33. Every curse of tragedy that has been taking people's lives before the day of their joy from generation to generation, your assignment is over, I command you to break now over my family in the name of Jesus Christ.
34. Every curse of tragedy that has been taking people's lives before the day of their joy from generation to generation, your assignment is over, I command you to break now over the life of my spouse in the name of Jesus Christ.
35. Every curse of tragedy that has been taking people's lives before the day of their joy from generation to generation, your assignment is over, I command you to break now over the life of my children in the name of Jesus Christ.

DAY FOUR

I SHALL CRY NO MORE

Passages To Read Before You Pray:
Revelation 21:4, Psalms 30, 34, 35, 70, 91, 140, 83

I stand on the word of God to claim my right as a child of the Kingdom, I cover myself in the blood of Jesus Christ, I cover my household and everything concerning me in the blood of Jesus Christ. I hereby charge this atmosphere by the blood of Jesus Christ and by the fire of the Holy Ghost. I command fresh fire of God to rest upon me now as in the day of Pentecost, let fresh anointing and new oil be released upon me now as I pray. I receive power and authority over the power and the kingdom of darkness, to root out and to pull down, to destroy and to throw down, to build and to plant; whatever I decree in this prayer shall be established; whatever I bind today shall be bound in heaven and whatever I loose today shall be loosed in heaven as it is written in the word of God. Let fresh fire of God be released on my prayer altar and my prayer life now, prince of Persia cannot hinder my prayer, territorial spirit of my neighborhood cannot hinder my prayer, household wickedness cannot hinder my prayer.

I can see my prayer attracting divine intervention. This is the day that the Lord has made, I will rejoice and be glad in it. This is the day that the Lord has chosen to set me free from any form of

bondage and break any form of curses upon my life; this is the day that I will receive a total and complete deliverance in every area of my life, today shall mark the beginning of a new thing in my life.

I am a child of God, born of the Spirit, redeemed by the blood of the Lamb. It is written concerning me that power and authority is given unto me over all devils and to cure diseases, I hereby take authority over any form of curses upon my life, be it ancestral, be it generational, be it demon-inflicted or self-inflicted; I command all curses upon my life to break now by the authority in the name of Jesus Christ. The Bible says, where the word of a king is, there is power; today I speak as a king with the authority and power of the King of kings, and I command every other power to bow in the name of Jesus Christ. I render any power behind any curse upon my life useless and ineffective; I overcome any form of distraction, spiritual laziness and slumber, before the end of this prayer session my testimonies shall manifest without delay by the power in the name of Jesus Christ. Amen!

PRAYER POINTS

1. O God my Father, thank you for being my God, my Father and my friend.
2. O God my Father, thank you for the privilege to know you and the power of the resurrection of Jesus Christ.
3. O God my Father, thank you for always being there for me and with me.
4. O God my Father, thank you for the great and mighty things that you are doing in my life.

5. O God my Father, thank you for your provision and protection over me and my household.
6. O God my Father, thank you for always answering my prayers.
7. I confess my sins before you today and I ask you to forgive me on the basis of your mercy, in the name of Jesus Christ.
8. Wash me clean today O Lord by the blood of Jesus Christ.
9. I cover myself and my household with the blood of Jesus Christ.
10. My prayers today will not go in vain; my prayers will produce the desired results in the name of Jesus Christ.
11. Every curse of tragedy that has been taking people's lives before the day of their joy from generation to generation, your assignment is over, I command you to break now over the life of my parents in the name of Jesus Christ.
12. Every curse of tragedy that has been taking people's lives before the day of their joy from generation to generation, your assignment is over, I command you to break now over the life of my siblings in the name of Jesus Christ.
13. Every curse of tragedy that has been taking people's lives before the day of their joy from generation to generation, your assignment is over, I command you to break now over the life of everyone around me in the name of Jesus Christ.
14. Every curse of tragedy that has been taking lives of men from generation to generation and causing their children to be left fatherless, I cancel your assignment over

family today, I command you to break now by the power in the name of Jesus Christ.
15. Every curse of tragedy that has been taking lives of men from generation to generation and causing their children to be left fatherless, I cancel your assignment over my life today, I command you to break now by the power in the name of Jesus Christ.
16. Every curse of tragedy that has been taking lives of men from generation to generation and causing their children to be left fatherless, I cancel your assignment over my spouse today, I command you to break now by the power in the name of Jesus Christ.
17. Every curse of tragedy that has been taking lives of men from generation to generation and causing their children to be left fatherless, I cancel your assignment over my marriage today, I command you to break now by the power in the name of Jesus Christ.
18. Every curse of tragedy that has been taking lives of men from generation to generation and causing their children to be left fatherless, I cancel your assignment over my children today, I command you to break now by the power in the name of Jesus Christ.
19. Every curse of tragedy that has been taking lives of women from generation to generation and causing their children to be left motherless, I cancel your assignment over my family today, I command you to break now by the power in the name of Jesus Christ.
20. Every curse of tragedy that has been taking lives of women from generation to generation and causing their children to be left motherless, I cancel your assignment over my life today, I command you to break now by the power in the name of Jesus Christ.

21. Every curse of tragedy that has been taking lives of women from generation to generation and causing their children to be left motherless, I cancel your assignment over my spouse today, I command you to break now by the power in the name of Jesus Christ.
22. Every curse of tragedy that has been taking lives of women from generation to generation and causing their children to be left motherless, I cancel your assignment over my marriage today, I command you to break now by the power in the name of Jesus Christ.
23. Every curse of tragedy that has been taking lives of women from generation to generation and causing their children to be left motherless, I cancel your assignment over my children today, I command you to break now by the power in the name of Jesus Christ.
24. Every curse of tragedy causing people to be homeless, I am not your candidate, I command you to break now by the power in the name of Jesus Christ.
25. Every curse of tragedy causing people to be homeless, my spouse is not your candidate, I command you to break now by the power in the name of Jesus Christ.
26. Every curse of tragedy causing people to be homeless, my children are not your candidate, I command you to break now by the power in the name of Jesus Christ.
27. Every curse of tragedy that turns laughter to tears, I am not your candidate, I command you to break now by the power in the name of Jesus Christ.
28. Every curse of tragedy that turns laughter to tears, my spouse is not your candidate, I command you to break now by the power in the name of Jesus Christ.

29. Every curse of tragedy that turns laughter to tears, my children are not your candidate, I command you to break now by the power in the name of Jesus Christ.
30. Today I decree by the power and authority in the blood of Jesus Christ, there shall be no tragedy in my home, in the name of Jesus Christ.
31. Today I decree by the power and authority in the blood of Jesus Christ, there shall be no tragedy in my family, in the name of Jesus Christ.
32. Today I decree by the power and authority in the blood of Jesus Christ, there shall be no tragedy concerning my spouse, in the name of Jesus Christ.
33. Today I decree by the power and authority in the blood of Jesus Christ, there shall be no tragedy concerning my children, in the name of Jesus Christ.
34. Today I decree by the power and authority in the blood of Jesus Christ, there shall be no tragedy concerning my parents, in the name of Jesus Christ.
35. Today I decree by the power and authority in the blood of Jesus Christ, there shall be no tragedy concerning my life, in the name of Jesus Christ.

DAY FIVE

THERE SHALL BE NO EVIL REPORT

Passages To Read Before You Pray:
Isaiah 41:10-13, Revelation 21:4, Isaiah 43:1-4, Psalms 30, 34, 35, 70, 91, 140, 83

I stand on the word of God to claim my right as a child of the Kingdom, I cover myself in the blood of Jesus Christ, I cover my household and everything concerning me in the blood of Jesus Christ. I hereby charge this atmosphere by the blood of Jesus Christ and by the fire of the Holy Ghost. I command fresh fire of God to rest upon me now as in the day of Pentecost, let fresh anointing and new oil be released upon me now as I pray. I receive power and authority over the power and the kingdom of darkness, to root out and to pull down, to destroy and to throw down, to build and to plant; whatever I decree in this prayer shall be established; whatever I bind today shall be bound in heaven and whatever I loose today shall be loosed in heaven as it is written in the word of God. Let fresh fire of God be released on my prayer altar and my prayer life now, prince of Persia cannot hinder my prayer, territorial spirit of my neighborhood cannot hinder my prayer, household wickedness cannot hinder my prayer.

I can see my prayer attracting divine intervention. This is the day that the Lord has made, I will rejoice and be glad in it. This is the

day that the Lord has chosen to set me free from any form of bondage and break any form of curses upon my life; this is the day that I will receive a total and complete deliverance in every area of my life, today shall mark the beginning of a new thing in my life.

I am a child of God, born of the Spirit, redeemed by the blood of the Lamb. It is written concerning me that power and authority is given unto me over all devils and to cure diseases, I hereby take authority over any form of curses upon my life, be it ancestral, be it generational, be it demon-inflicted or self-inflicted; I command all curses upon my life to break now by the authority in the name of Jesus Christ. The Bible says, where the word of a king is, there is power; today I speak as a king with the authority and power of the King of kings, and I command every other power to bow in the name of Jesus Christ. I render any power behind any curse upon my life useless and ineffective; I overcome any form of distraction, spiritual laziness and slumber, before the end of this prayer session my testimonies shall manifest without delay by the power in the name of Jesus Christ. Amen!

PRAYER POINTS

1. O God my Father, thank you for being my God, my Father and my friend.
2. O God my Father, thank you for the privilege to know you and the power of the resurrection of Jesus Christ.
3. O God my Father, thank you for always being there for me and with me.

4. O God my Father, thank you for the great and mighty things that you are doing in my life.
5. O God my Father, thank you for your provision and protection over me and my household.
6. O God my Father, thank you for always answering my prayers.
7. I confess my sins before you today and I ask you to forgive me on the basis of your mercy, in the name of Jesus Christ.
8. Wash me clean today O Lord by the blood of Jesus Christ.
9. I cover myself and my household with the blood of Jesus Christ.
10. My prayers today will not go in vain; my prayers will produce the desired results in the name of Jesus Christ.
11. Today I decree by the power and authority in the blood of Jesus Christ, there shall be no tragedy in any area of my interest, in the name of Jesus Christ.
12. Today I decree by the power and authority in the blood of Jesus Christ, there shall be no evil report in my home, in the name of Jesus Christ.
13. Today I decree by the power and authority in the blood of Jesus Christ, there shall be no evil report in my family, in the name of Jesus Christ.
14. Today I decree by the power and authority in the blood of Jesus Christ, there shall be no evil report in my marriage, in the name of Jesus Christ.
15. Today I decree by the power and authority in the blood of Jesus Christ, there shall be no evil report concerning my spouse, in the name of Jesus Christ.

16. Today I decree by the power and authority in the blood of Jesus Christ, there shall be no evil report concerning my children, in the name of Jesus Christ.
17. Today I decree by the power and authority in the blood of Jesus Christ, there shall be no evil report concerning my parents, in the name of Jesus Christ.
18. Today I decree by the power and authority in the blood of Jesus Christ, there shall be no evil report concerning my life, in the name of Jesus Christ.
19. Today I decree by the power and authority in the blood of Jesus Christ, there shall be no evil report concerning my business, in the name of Jesus Christ.
20. Today I decree by the power and authority in the blood of Jesus Christ, there shall be no evil report in any area of my interest, in the name of Jesus Christ.
21. Today I decree by the power and authority in the blood of Jesus Christ that the noise of crying and wailing shall not be heard in my house, in the name of Jesus Christ.
22. Every cycle of tragedy in my life, enough is enough, I command you to break now by the power in the name of Jesus Christ.
23. Every cycle of tragedy in my family, enough is enough, I command you to break now by the power in the name of Jesus Christ.
24. Every cycle of tragedy affecting the life of my spouse, enough is enough, I command you to break now by the power in the name of Jesus Christ.
25. Every cycle of tragedy affecting the life of my children, enough is enough, I command you t break now by the power in the name of Jesus Christ.

26. Every cycle of tragedy in the life of my parents, enough of enough, I command you to break now by the power in the name of Jesus Christ.
27. Every cycle of tragedy affecting my progress, enough is enough, I command you to break now by the power in the name of Jesus Christ.
28. Every cycle of tragedy affecting my fruitfulness, enough is enough, I command you to break now by the power in the name of Jesus Christ.
29. Every cycle of tragedy causing me to live a roller-coaster life, enough is enough, I command you to break right now by the power in the name of Jesus Christ.
30. O God my Father, let season of tragedy end now and let season of rejoicing begin, in the name of Jesus Christ.
31. O God my Father, let season of tragedy end now and let season of celebration begin, in the name of Jesus Christ.
32. O God my Father, let season of weeping end now and let season of laughter begin, in the name of Jesus Christ.
33. Today I decree that the joy of the Lord shall be strength in the name of Jesus Christ.
34. This year and all the days of my life, I shall have no reason to cry in the name of Jesus Christ.
35. My God is doing new things in my life, therefore I will laugh a new laugh, dance a new dance, sing a new song, and everyone around me will celebrate with me in the name of Jesus Christ.

Notes

Notes

Printed in Great Britain
by Amazon